The World
of the Dog

ESTHER J.J. VERHOEF-VERHALLEN

 **REBO**
PRODUCTIONS

© 1996 Zuid Boekprodukties, Lisse
© 1997 Published by Rebo Productions Ltd
Cover design: Ton Wienbelt, The Netherlands
Photo editor: Marieke Uiterwijk
Photographs: Esther J.J. Verhoef-Verhallen
Production: TextCase, The Netherlands
Translation: Saskia Barker for
First Edition Translations Ltd, Cambridge, UK
Typesetting: Hof&Land Typografie, The Netherlands

ISBN: 1 901094 472

Contents

CHAPTER I

The origins of the domesticated dog

When we consider the enormous diversity in the appearance of modern breeds of dog, it can be difficult to believe that all of them are descended from the wolf. Most scientists agree that the dog's original ancestor could only have been the wolf, although there are also those who have different opinions.

There is, however, no incontrovertible proof of the origins of domestic dogs, and it is interesting to take a look at the opposing opinions.

For many years people believed that wolves were blood-thirsty, fearless killers, prepared to attack humans. For that reason, they have been hunted by man for centuries and their numbers have been dramatically reduced.

Neapolitan Mastiff (Mastino Napolitano)

The wolf as ancestor

Scientists who believe that our domestic dogs are descended from wolves base this on, very complex genetic studies, and on the behaviour of the dog, which is broadly similar to that of the wolf. Dogs, like wolves, are pack animals and can manage on their own only with difficulty or not at all.

This may explain how it is that they have adapted reasonably easily to living with people, in contrast to the largely solitary lifestyle of cats. Further, the body language dogs use to communicate with people and with other dogs strongly resembles the body language of wolves. For example, some dogs howl just as wolves do.

Swedish Vallhund. Dogs frequently howl because they feel lonely and want company

Researchers into animal behaviour have been able to determine that one wolf, usually a juvenile, stays in a safe 'rendez-vous' site with the pack's cubs while the others go out hunting. That juvenile left in charge would usually warn the rest of the pack by howling if danger should threaten the cubs.

When this wolf howls, the rest of the pack return to the camp to come to its aid. If the juvenile wolf did not report danger, or failed to protect the cubs, he would likely be driven from the pack or even killed.

This kind of howling can also be observed in many domesticated dogs. Insecure or older dogs will sometimes howl when they are left alone. Because we are absent they feel a sense of responsibility but, because they may sense instinctively that they would not be strong enough to defend themselves, they will often howl to call us back. Howling sometimes has a more social meaning. It can be very infec-

tious and, when a wolf or dog howls, others will react by howling in sympathy. The sound they make can sometimes be heard for long distances.

This kind of howling has a quite different function. It is a form of communication through which the animals advise each other of their position. Howling together strengthens their sense of community and tells other groups of dogs about territory occupation.

There are other behaviours which wolves and dogs share. Chapter 6 (Canine Behaviour) discusses further examples.

Wolves and humans

The first wolf to attach himself to primitive humanity may have been a lone juvenile wolf who did so of his own free will, preferring

The Siberian Husky strongly resembles a wolf. Its thick coat protects it well against the cold

the companionship and safety of a group of people to his own, uncertain, lonely existence. For the wolf, life in the vicinity of humans meant that he was certain of his daily ration. He would have sensed instinctively that his chances of survival were slender if he left. Primitive humans may have noticed that a wolf eating left-overs from their meals was useful.

A wolf was also capable of warning them of approaching danger and was helpful in the hunt. People would therefore have tolerated the wolf's presence in their camp. Evidence

Chow-chow puppy

shows that some wolves altered their lifestyles to live with humans in early villages about 10,000 years ago. Domestication did not occur overnight, but cooperation between the two species is believed to have occurred after an aggregation of juvenile, perhaps lone, wolves in village dumps. Man probably ate many of these wolves, but others were encouraged to

The Inuit sometimes crossed their sledge dogs with wolves to produce stronger and larger dogs. The Alaskan Malamute is probably descended from one such cross

guard, hunt and herd. Selecting for behaviour characteristics produced changes in physical appearance and behaviour.

Crosses between dogs and wolves

Many breeds of dog look similar to wolves, and it safe to say that their physical appearance is less physically altered than some of

Right: German Shepherd Dog

Below: The small Griffon Bruxellois is a charming little hound that can easily be kept as a pet

the other breeds. The German Shepherd Dog and the various breeds of Arctic dog are examples of dogs that closer in appearance to their wolf forebears.

The Inuit sometimes let bitches be covered by wolves, the intention being to produce bigger, stronger dogs, better able to do heavy work.

They would tie up a bitch on heat in a place near to the 'camp' of a pack of wolves. Some-

Left: The Saarloos Wolfhound was bred by crossing German Shepherds with wolves

Below: This Cirneco Dell'Etna is enjoying the spring sunshine with her owner and her companions. The Cirneco Dell'Etna is a half-greyhound: it has sharp sight and hearing as well as a good nose

times this went well: the bitch dropped a litter of puppies with the desired attributes. However, these experiments were not always without danger.

The bitch might be eaten by a larger predator, or a dominant and irritable she-wolf might could find her a threat.

Not all crosses between wolves and dogs originated in this rather barbaric way. The Saarloos Wolfhound is a recent Dutch breed, devel-oped from wolves and German Shepherds. A Dutchman, Leendert Saarloos, was convinced that the domestic dog (especially his favourite breed, the German Shepherd Dog) had too many genetic weaknesses, which he attributed to over-domestication.

By introducing wolf blood he hoped to create a new breed that had all the positive attributes of the German Shepherd Dog but without its genetic weaknesses. In the event he was only

partially successful. All of its descendants have the wolf's highly developed sense of flight which means that they cannot be used for the purposes Leendert Saarloos had in mind – such as police work, for example. As pets, however, the animals are an excellent choice. They are very sociable and enjoy the company of other pets, including dogs. They are also ideal companions for children. This breed is also unusually healthy.

Today, the Saarloos Wolfhound is one of the few breeds that has remained free of hereditary weaknesses – and for this the credit must go to the keen breeders who have continued the work of Saarloos.

In 1975 the Saarloos Wolfhound was finally recognised as an official breed – six years after the death of its original breeder.

The Netherlands is not the only country to produce a new breed of dog in this way. Although fewer in numbers, there is a similar breed in the Czech Republic – the Czech Wolfhound.

The influence of other wild canines

Many of the breeds developed in Europe and America resemble the wolf quite closely. Their build, behaviour and coat confirm their ancestry.

In other parts of the world – for example Africa – we tend to see short-haired, lightly built dogs with different hunting patterns.

These animals are less obviously descended from the thick-coated, heavily built wolf. Since jackals and coyote are numerous in the

Italian Greyhounds. Mummified remains of this type of dog have been found in Egyptian graves

Basenji

climate, these mutations were better able to survive than the more wolf-like dogs.

However, some scientists do not accept this, and continue to look for proof of other forebears in old manuscripts and archaeological finds from ancient cultures. These investigations indicated that the famous Egyptian Pharaoh, Tutankhamon, owned a dog that was a cross between a local wild dog and a jackal.

In Egypt, the dog had a religious role – representing Anubis, guardian of the dead. It had adjusted well to life at court and was frequently used to hunt gazelles. The numerous

areas where these dogs are found, it may be possible that these are their original ancestors.

This issue has kept scientists busy for years. Those who held that the wolf was the only real ancestor of all domestic dogs presented the argument that the African breeds could be mutations of more wolf-like dogs. Because their thinner coats made them more suitable for life in the dry and very warm African

Above: Otterhounds are very sociable dogs with an excellent nose

Hovawarts come in three colours: black, golden, and black and tan

Above: Golden Retriever

paintings of such dogs found in Egyptian tombs may indicate that the Egyptians crossed breeds to produce a superior dog. Alternatively, others argue that the breed was simply a 'show' dog, and that the Egyptians had no concept of 'breeds'.

Mummified specimens have also been discovered. Although opinion continues to be divided, these finds have offered food for thought. It is possible that the influence of other wild dogs in addition to that of the wolf led to the development of modern breeds.

Left: Berger Picard

Right: The Bull Mastiff is the product of crossing the Mastiff with the English Bulldog. These dogs used to accompany British gamekeepers when they made their nightly patrols of the woods

Dog breeds in ancient Egypt

Tutankamon's dog was likely a Pharaoh Hound. Perpetuated by enthusiasts, the Pharaoh Hound does still exist today and, at the beginning of this century, it was officially recognised as a breed.

Closely related to the Pharaoh Hound are the Sicilian Hound (Cirnecco Dell' Etna) and the Ibizan Hound (Podenco Ibicenco). These dogs share the same capacity to hunt by scent as well as by sight and sharp hearing. When these dogs smell their quarry, they stand up on their hind-legs to watch it. All wolves and dogs hunt using all of their senses, but some were selected for enhanced ability to follow scents, or to see at a distance. Usually these enhanced senses were at the cost of other sensory acuteness or physical abilities.

Smooth-haired standard Dachshund.
Dachshunds are very independent and brave and are used to hunt rabbits

The Basenji, a breed used in Africa as a hunting and guard dog, also has its own special way of hunting. There have been several attempts to introduce these dogs to Europe but it was difficult at first to keep them alive in a more temperate climate.

Most of the Basenjis imported from Africa became ill and quickly died. By selective breeding with stronger dogs, Basenjis are today a healthy breed.

One of the Basenjis' remarkable qualities is that it does not bark. Instead it produces a kind of yodelling sound, which is unknown in any other dog.

Mutations and selection

It is possible that mutations (spontaneous changes in an animal's genes) are the reason that there are now so many different breeds of dog. Mutations still occur occasionally, as in

The Neapolitan Mastiff (Mastino Napolitano) is a natural guard dog. It will guard its owners and their property with its life

Left: This dog is the result of "an affair" between a sledge dog and a sheep dog

the case of white tigers or giraffes. In the wild, such animals would have difficulty surviving, because their light-coloured coat is too visible in their environment.

However, when such animals are kept in captivity they can be protected, and eventually a new breed might develop. Although in the past people knew very little about genetics, they were nevertheless able to breed dogs with the qualities they found useful. Dogs that proved to be better equipped for particular work were crossed with each other so that gradually specialised breeds were developed. In time, such selections have led to different kinds of hunting dogs, dogs to guard flocks, herding dogs and guard dogs. In general, it is not recommended that you breed two dogs with very different backgrounds as it will not be possible to predict the character of their descendants.

Breeds developed from a spontaneous mutation

A good example of a breed developed by the chance mutation of selective breeding is the Dachshund. Having short legs is not a natural canine characteristic but proved to be very useful when hunting below ground. Dogs with short legs are so low-slung that they are able to follow their quarry deep into its hole.

CHAPTER 2

Choosing a dog

Whatever dog you choose, it is important not to rush the decision because your new companion is certainly not a disposable item. If you bear this in mind it is clear that the choice and purchase of a dog is not a matter to be undertaken lightly.

Initial considerations

Before buying an adult dog or puppy, you will need to take account of your domestic arrangements. The animal will become a member of your family for ten years or more and it will influence your daily activities.

You should ask yourself whether you have enough time for its care. If you have only a little time, then a dog requiring, for example,

Right: Rough-coated Dutch Sheepdogs are uncomplicated, obedient family dogs. Dutch Sheepdogs can be smooth, rough, and long coated

Boston Terrier

extensive grooming, is not a sensible choice. There are numerous other such questions you must ask yourself before deciding to buy. Will you or another member of your family be as happy to take the dog for its daily walk when the novelty has worn off? It is also important to remember that dogs can be expensive to feed; large dogs in particular can make a significant dent in your family's budget.

Apart from food there are inoculations, worming, flea-powders, and the cost of dog grooming. Only if you are quite certain that you have carefully considered all these questions should you decide which breed, or possibly mongrel, takes your fancy.

A pedigree dog

If you choose a pedigree dog you can be more certain of its size and character than if you choose a mongrel. Each breed has its own characteristics. Make a list of what you expect from your new companion. Try not to concentrate too much on appearance: you will quickly get used to a beautiful-looking animal but if the dog has a character that doesn't fit your domestic situation you will never get along. In the end, you will find a breed that

Left: Phalene

Schnauzers are easily trained and good with children

The Basset Fauve de Bretagne is a friendly family dog that values the company of other dogs

satisfies your requirements not only in terms of character but also in terms of its appearance; after all, there are almost 150 different breeds of dog to choose from.

Your list should include whether the dog needs to be able to guard, how much time you wish to spend grooming it, how large or how small the dog must be (dependent of course on the size of your home), and whether it is important to you that the dog can be easily trained or if you would appreciate a dog with a greater degree of independence.

If you already have pets, or children, it is important that the newcomer should be sociable. Not all breeds are suitable for sharing the house with cats or children! Finally, the dog's need for exercise is very important.

The Friesian Staby or Stabyhoun is a very friendly and obedient household companion

Any dog, but especially an active hunting dog or greyhound, should not be condemned simply to walking round the block three times a day. Most dogs need a good run daily, preferably in open space.

With your own list in mind, you could study books about pedigree dogs or talk to enthusiasts and breeders. You will need to be well equipped with information to make an informed choice. Many people choose a popular breed because they are unaware that other breeds exist, or because they have difficulty finding breeders of less well-known dogs. It is worth asking your local dog club whether they could give you advice. And, of course, many different breeds can be seen at large dog shows.

Buying a pedigree dog

You should never buy a pedigree dog from the first breeder who happens to have a litter of

Borzois are generally not ideal companions for young children. However, there are always exceptions

Azawakhs are not everyone's kind of dog on account of their strong independent characters

puppies. Since the breeding of pedigree dogs can be quite a lucrative business, there are always people who breed only for profit without paying attention to the health and character of the parents and puppies. It is a good idea to contact the breed society of your chosen dog.

Almost every breed has this kind of society. The members will give you objective advice and the addresses or telephone numbers of approved and often registered breeders.

Approved breeders will do everything they can to breed the healthiest and most beautiful dogs possible and will leave little to chance.

Mongrels

If the precise breed doesn't matter because you are just looking for a friendly companion and do not intend to show or breed from your dog, you could consider acquiring a mongrel. Mongrels are frequently cheap and certainly no less fun or charming than a pedigree dog. They are often available in dog homes but your local newspaper will also carry regular advertisements for mongrel puppies. You may know somebody in your area with a litter for sale.

Although the cheaper price of such a puppy may be the deciding factor in your choice, you should consider the fact that mongrels do have

Above: The Labrador Retriever is a very friendly and obedient dog

The Field Spaniel is a hunting dog used to flush out game and to retrieve it. One of the most obedient of the spaniels, it also makes a loyal companion

their disadvantages. But mongrels are a popular choice, and at least 40 percent of dog owners have a crossbreed or a mongrel.

You cannot show a mongrel or even a pedigree dog without registration certificates. They are, however, very welcome at agility, obedience, and fly-ball competitions.

A dog from an animal rescue centre

It shows a great deal of love to adopt a dog from a rescue centre. These centres are usually full of dogs waiting for a new home. You may well find the perfect dog for you and your family there. People sometimes think that all rescue-centre dogs are dogs with an infamous past, but this is not always the case. Many friendly, healthy, and well brought-up dogs wait in rescue centres for new owners. Do beware of dogs with behaviour or control problems – neither of which may be insurmountable, but certainly a consideration when buying a dog from a rescue centre.

There are many reasons why dogs end up in rescue centre. Perhaps the previous owner had to go back to work or went into an old people's home. Others may have ended up there as a result of divorce. The rescue centre

West Highland White Terriers need affectionate but firm training as they can be very independent

Below: Big dogs, such as these Mastiffs, need a lot of space

will gladly give you information about the dog's background.

Dog or bitch?

Whether you prefer a dog or bitch is a matter of personal choice. Both sexes have their pros and cons.
A bitch will generally go 'into heat' twice a year. When they are in heat, bitches are open to the advances of dogs and you will need to

Animal rescue centres are usually full of dogs waiting for new homes

Right: This little dog proves that mongrels can be unusually beautiful

Below: This cross-breed clearly has fox terrier blood, which will make him a lively addition to your household

Three generations of Pugs. Pugs are known to have existed in China before the birth of Christ.
In the Middle Ages, they were imported into Europe.
They are affectionate little dogs that have difficulty getting used to new owners

be extra vigilant if you don't want to be surprised by an unwanted litter. If this poses a problem for you, you may decide in discussion with your veterinary surgeon to sterilise your bitch (which is actually called spaying or a hysterectomy).

If you do not intend to breed from your bitch it is advisable to have her sterilised. Older, unsterilised bitches may suffer from inflammation of the uterus, which can sometimes be life-threatening.

Male dogs can breed from about ten months, and are sexually active all year round, picking up the scent given off by any bitch in season. If they detect a potentially interesting smell they may become very restless and may go after it.

Smooth coated Chihuahua puppies. Chihuahuas are the smallest breed of dog, sometimes weighing no more than 1kg (2lb)

The differences between a dog and a bitch are quite noticeable during their daily walks. Dogs are much more likely to leave their scent-markers at any available point along their path and may react somewhat aggressively to other dogs. Bitches usually urinate only once during a walk and are generally also easier with other dogs.

In more aggressive breeds, the male can become a good and reliable guard dog but will require a firm owner. In gentler breeds, the differences between the sexes can be less pronounced.

Large or small dog?

Whether you would be better with a large or small dog or possibly one in between depends on your situation. If you live in a small house and are not particularly energetic, you and the dog will be happier if you decide on a small breed. Small breeds not only need less space but also cost considerably less in food and care. It is also easier to travel with a small dog.

Large dogs or smaller, aggressive dogs, have the distinct advantage in that they generally

The Great Dane, together with the Irish Wolfhound, are the largest breeds. They can be more than one metre at the shoulder, but dogs must be at least 80cm (30in) tall

Like all Collies, this puppy will be highly intelligent and learn fast

terrify burglars. Alternatively, everything concerning a large dog is more expensive: not just trimming it and feeding it but also visits to the veterinary surgeon will be more expensive because the dosages of any medication will be larger. It is sometimes said that a large dog should not be kept in an apartment but should live in a large house with a garden. This is only partly true.

If a large dog in an apartment gets sufficient exercise he will certainly be much happier than his more generously accommodated relation who never gets further than his garden. If you live in an apartment and decide to have a large dog you will need to take account of the fact that it will grow very quickly.
In the first two years of life, the dog's bones,

When this Tibetan Mastiff puppy grows up, it will be a
gentle watchdog with a pronounced character

muscles, and tendons adapt a great deal. If there is no lift in the building where you live, remember that the dog will have to negotiate the stairs, which will put added strain on his growing body.

Puppy or adult dog?

Another decision is whether to purchase a puppy or an adult dog. You can of course train a puppy to suit your own needs, but you may also make mistakes in its training, which may be difficult to reverse later.

An older dog will need rather more time to settle in, but if it has already received a good foundation training it will be house-trained and will have outgrown all its puppy and adolescent foibles.
If you do buy an older dog it is important that you should be aware of its history. For

themselves with the care of the animals as well as their owners. This is, of course, highly regrettable. Parting owner from loyal dog in such circumstances can be painful and traumatic for both.

The situation might be different if those responsible for running the homes were aware of the fact that elderly people who are used to caring for a pet are frequently more healthy than others. It has been proved that stroking a dog or cat has a significant therapeutic effect. Dog owners also seem to have relatively fewer heart problems than people without animals – largely because they are used to regular exercise with their dog. Owning a dog may also reduce loneliness – not only because they can be good company, but also because a dog is frequently an excuse to start up a conversation with a stranger.

Pets are prohibited in many old people's homes

example, is he for sale because of his unpleasant character or does his owner not have time to groom him? Sometimes breeders offer bitches for sale that are no longer fertile or that carry hereditary faults so that they cannot be used for breeding.

Such dogs may develop into excellent family pets, but, if the breeder keeps his dogs outside in kennels, they may not be housetrained and may have difficulty adapting to the life of a household pet.

Older people and dogs

Many retirement homes will not accept pets. One of the reasons for this is that the people who run the homes have no time to concern

Bolognese dogs do not moult, but their coat nevertheless requires daily care

CHAPTER 3

Training

If you do not want your dog to bark at the window or pull on the lead whenever you take it for a walk, you will need to spend some time training your puppy.

Right: The English Springer Spaniel is a pleasant and obedient family dog, and an all-round hunting hound. This is a very old breed that has probably been known by the same name since 1600

This French Bulldog has learnt to walk beside its owner without pulling at the lead

Socialisation phase

In the first twelve to fourteen weeks of its life the puppy will need to absorb a great many different impressions if it is to grow into a well-balanced, agreeable family dog. Very important for the development of a dog's character are, among others periods, the socialisation phase.

Just before the socialising period, which begins at about the fifth week is an important stage of development which some people call 'imprinting'. This stage runs from the onset of sensory awareness (sight and sound) and mobility to the onset of neophobic responses at the end of the fifth week, and throughout this time your puppy will be particularly open to influences, and is extremely susceptible to environmental influences.

A puppy that spent this phase in isolation, not coming into contact with everyday things or with other dogs, people, and animals, may, for the rest of its life, react fearfully to its daily environment. Such a miserable animal may view every approach from a human being or another dog as a threat and, as a result, the animal can develop apathetic or aggressive behaviour. A dog that has been neglected in this phase of its life will need a great deal of affection, patience, and dedication.

After five weeks your puppy enters the socialisation phase, which lasts until approximately

The Shar Pei is an old Chinese breed. Characteristic of the breed are the deep wrinkles, which should be less pronounced in adult dogs than in puppies

the fourteenth week. During this phase your puppy learns to deal with dogs and other pets, strangers and children. He will also learn to deal with heavy traffic, noise indoors and out, and numerous events which occur in their daily lives. The difference between this phase and the 'imprinting' phase is that, unlike a dog that has been badly or scarcely imprinted, the behaviour of a poorly socialised dog can usually be adjusted with patience.

Most puppies will leave the litter for their new owners at between eight and twelve weeks of age. A good breeder will have ensured that the puppies have received an a good introduction to life and to their surroundings.
Thereafter it is up to you to ensure that, in the next important phase of its life, your puppy becomes as sociable as possible.

This appealing Havanese puppy is a member of the Bichon family. These dogs do not moult

Socialisation in practice

To ensure that your puppy grows up sociably, it is a good idea to take it frequently to places where it can familiarise itself with many different sensations. Introduce it to other

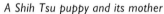

A Shih Tsu puppy and its mother

animals, for example at a children's model farm. To reduce the risk of tragic accidents later, you should introduce your puppy to children as soon as possible. You could, for example, introduce him to local children in the park or playground. Even if you think you will never travel with your dog by train or visit someone in an apartment that will mean using a lift, it is still advisable to familiarise your dog with such things. During this familiarisation process, try to give your puppy confidence and encouragement.

Many experts believe that it is not appropriate to comfort your dog in new situations, which may confirm his belief that there is something to fear. If the dog has a negative or even traumatic experience it may influence the way it reacts to other dogs and cats when he has grown up. An anxious reaction on your part will increase your puppy's fear. The more your puppy sees, hears, touches and tastes, the

The owner of these Dobermanns also keeps fowl. By spending a lot of time and effort socialising and training his dogs, he has ensured that they live together harmoniously

Some experts believe that it is good for children to grow up with one or more dogs

more it meets and plays with other dogs, children and adults, the better equipped it will be to cope with adult life. Research has proved that dogs that are not introduced to everyday activities early on, such as walking beside traffic, may grow fearful of such things and suffer behavioural problems later on.

Once puppies have made it safely through the initial important phases, they will have a good foundation for the rest of their lives.

Left: A Rottweiler puppy

Right: Bull Terrier

The name of the small Schipperke is derived from the Belgian word 'scheper', meaning shepherd. The breed therefore has nothing to do with ships

The Tibetan Spaniel is a cheerful intelligent dog

House-training

Many people, quite unnecessarily, dread house-training a puppy. Dogs have an excellent sense of smell and they are creatures of habit. If you use these two facts as your point of departure in house-training, your dog will soon realise what you want of him. Encourage him to do his business in the same place. Your dog will probably smell what he did there before and, out of habit, do it there again. Take your puppy into the garden at regular intervals and stay with it until it has emptied either its bladder or bowels.

Don't forget to reward it enthusiastically whenever it relieves itself outside. Dogs are very sensitive to their owner's mood and intonation of voice. They are very keen to do things which meet with your approval, not least because that way they expect to be stroked or reminded in some other way that they are loved. Try not to let your puppy relieve itself indoors. You will need to keep a close eye on him for the first few weeks.

A good rule of thumb is to take the puppy outside every time it has been asleep, or after a meal, or after it has been playing.

If your puppy circles round with its nose close to the ground, as though looking for something, it is probably looking for somewhere to relieve itself. Should your puppy have an acci-

> ### TIP
> **Puppies will almost always want to relieve themselves first thing in the morning, so always take them out at this time. Rubbing your dog's nose in its own mess will not solve the problem of accidents. Wait for the next opportunity when your puppy squats on the floor and firmly carry it through to the garden.**

dent, be calm but firm. If you speak very severely to a puppy when you catch it making a puddle, it could get the idea that it is not allowed to relieve itself when you are watching.

It will then start to look for less obvious places and will not dare relieve himself at all outside if you are watching. Always clean up accidents very carefully with strong-smelling disinfectant so that the puppy will not recognise the soiled area as a suitable toilet.

Don't punish a puppy who has had an accident, for it will grow up frightened and insecure. During the day, it is relatively straightforward to prevent your dog from relieving itself indoors, but this is more difficult at night. Take it for a good walk as late as possible before going to bed. And, just as you would with a new baby, or a child potty-training, you will probably have to wake up in the night to take it outside.

Don't fall into the trap of denying your puppy food or water at night. Growing puppies need plenty to eat and drink, and if you deny them either they may not develop properly. They may also learn to see nighttime as a period of unhappiness rather than a good opportunity to sleep.

The best advice is to be patient. House-training takes some time, and there are bound to be accidents along the way. Be firm but kind, and set up a routine that your dog can understand.

If you take your puppy to the same place every time, it will become house-trained more quickly

Above: The Kooiker is a Dutch breed specially developed to help when hunting for ducks

The Papillon or Butterfly Dog. There is also a kind with dropped ears, the Phalene, which is sometimes known as the Moth Dog

Training a dog

Every dog needs to understand a number of basic rules in order to become a pleasant companion. Some people consider this type of training to be 'drilling' and do not feel comfortable imposing their own will on their dogs.

If you are concerned about this, remember that dogs like doing things for their owners. Almost all dogs were originally working dogs and they do become bored if they have nothing constructive to do. Regardless of its breed, any dog that is taken out three times a day but left to its own devices for the rest of the time is likely to be unhappy. It is also much more pleasant for you to have a dog that obeys commands or requests. No one wants a dog that always pulls on the lead, stands on the windowsill barking at passers-by, or behaves aggressively to children.

Be Consistent

The most important thing in training a dog is to be consistent and to ensure that you have effective communication. Being consistent means establishing rules that are never broken. For example, if the dog is not permitted on the sofa you should not make special allowances, even when it is ill. Talk to your dog, and use the same firm instructions each time. Make sure your dog understands you, and if he does not, try to find another way to communicate your rules.

If you do not want the dog to jump up at you, never permit it to do so, even in fun. If future

Golden Retriever

Three of these dogs are rescue cases that were taken in as adult dogs, and they have all learned a great deal with good training

It is good practice to train a puppy to sit at the edge of the sidewalk before crossing the road

Curly-coated Retrievers are usually black, but liver, like this dog, is also acceptable

Right: English Setters

he is told off for the same behaviour on a later occasion, he will not understand at all. You cannot expect your dog to appreciate the subtle differences that are so obvious to humans.

Consistency in all things also means consistency in training. Never accept your dog's

TIP

It is good practice to train a puppy to sit at the edge of the sidewalk. This will not only give you the opportunity to look around carefully before crossing the road but you will also reduce the chances of your dog simply running across the road without looking.

failure to obey a command or only partial obedience. For example, if your dog finally sits after you have given it the command to lie down, you should never accept this as sufficient, not even if you are becoming frustrated. In the early days, your dog may not always understand what you want him to do and will make mistakes. Speak your commands in conjunction with hand movements. Initially your dog will understand your words only if accompanied by a physical demonstration. When you are training your dog, choose a relatively quiet place, free from distractions. When training your dog, it will need lots of reassurance and gentle encouragement.

A Dutch Smoushond

Right: The Newfoundland may be brown or black, and occasionally black and white

Reward-based training is often successful. Begin by teaching your puppy simple skills such as how to walk to heel, how to sit when commanded, how to stay or to life down. Always acknowledge obedience either with food treats, patting of the head or verbal praise.

Teach your puppy its name so that it comes to you every time it is called. Always use a friendly, reassuring tone and do not use the name in reprimand. Be consistent and patient and your dog will eventually learn what you expect of it.

Even if you live alone with a dog it can be quite demanding to be consistent. In a family, all members should follow the same rules.

Basic concepts

Every dog must learn how to walk quietly on the lead without pulling or picking fights with other dogs. There are also a number of commands he will need to obey. To teach your dog to walk to heel, you should shorten your dog's lead sufficiently for it to walk alongside you, its right shoulder at your left leg. Walk calmly in a straight line, repeating the word 'heel' in a firm voice. Check from time to time that your dog is not falling behind or racing ahead.

Teach your dog to sit when he has mastered the art of walking to heel. Apply firm but gentle pressure on the dog's back and repeat the word 'sit'. To begin with, speak this command in conjunction with the hand movement.It will soon learn to understand the words alone.

Assistance in training

It is perfectly possible, and indeed enjoyable, to train your dog.yourself. If you remain con-

The Saint Bernard was once used to find and rescue stranded travellers

basic exercises for a German Shepherd Dog, which frequently master such commands within a week.

The local dog association will also be of help if you have bought an older dog. It's an old saying that old dogs cannot learn new tricks, but this is not true.

Old dogs may not learn as quickly as puppies but, with good training and much enthusiasm, it is possible to teach an older dog a great deal. Remember that an older dog will tire more easily than a puppy and a rigorous routine may not be advisable. Training will make your dog feel secure and it will know its boundaries.

Children and dogs

sistent and establish good communication channels with your dog, training can be very straightforward. If you have little experience of training dogs or lack confidence, it is best to contact a local dog club. These associations regularly provide puppy training courses, as well as other kinds of training. The courses are usually not expensive because they need to be accessible to all. A professional trainer will teach you how best to react to your dog's behaviour. Most people and their dogs look forward to the weekly lesson, which can be informative and frequently great fun.

Lifelong friendships are often forged at such associations – and not only among the dogs. If you have a rare breed, it may be worthwhile enquiring whether the instructors know about the breed. Every breed has its own characteristics, and an obliging and possibly shy dog will need to be treated quite differently from a cocky one. In addition, not all breeds are equally quick on the uptake, nor do they all have the same desire to obey. It is a considerable achievement for an Afghan hound to sit or lie down on command, whereas these are

Research has shown that it is very good for children to grow up with one or more dogs. By taking care of a dog, a child will learn early in life what it means to be responsible for a totally dependent living being. There can be very close bonds between children and dogs, which adults should not underestimate Dogs can also be a very loyal and supportive friend for a child – and most dogs demand little more than fun and affection in return.

Most importantly, dogs don't ask questions, and can provide a warm and sympathetic companion in a time of need. But however kind and gentle some dogs can be, it is always sensible to exercise a certain caution. Never leave a dog alone with young children, particularly with children to whom it is unaccustomed. Dogs and children should only be allowed out alone together if the child can master the dog spiritually as well as physically. This depends not only on the child but also on the size and character of the dog. If the child has not acquired sufficient mastery of the dog or has not yet developed a sufficient sense of responsibility, accidents are possible. Further, very young children can inadvertently hurt a dog through play or inappropriate training. This could force the dog to defend itself, with all the consequences of such an action.

Teach a child always to call a dog to him or her and not to walk towards the dog. In dog language, walking towards a dog means that the child is inferior to the dog. Never let a young child wrestle with any dog.

If the dog was in the house before the child, you must stop the dog seeing the new child as an interloper and hence becoming jealous. Your dog will have to learn that things will be different in the household. As long as you are careful not to ignore the dog, which will cause it to see the child as competition for resources and affection, or even position in the home, your dog can learn to enjoy a new family member and accept a baby or child more quickly. A dog needs to know that this major change in the family will not have negative consequences for him. Some experts advise

asking visitors to provide a gift for the dog as well as the new baby, but as long as you show a consistent level of affection and respect for your dog, this is probably unnecessary. Let your dog know that it is still part of the family and as important to you as it ever was. Teach it new rules to make life easier, but be fair and gentle and it will respond in kind.

TIP

Most dogs love water and are keen swimmers. Sometimes a dog needs a little encouragement because it may still be a little apprehensive about water. Most dogs will not be able to resist the temptation to follow your example if you go into the water yourself.

Never throw a frightened dog into the water; the fright could cause it to run away and refuse to be caught. There is also the possibility that it will not only lose its trust in you but also never dare to swim again.

Necessary equipment

Before you bring home your new dog, there are certain things you should already have in the house. This chapter will cover those items which you need to buy in advance.

Baskets

Your dog will need a fixed place to which it can retire if it is tired of playing and where it can sleep undisturbed. Generally a basket is used for this purpose. Baskets come in different sizes and different materials.

Cane baskets are usually not suitable for young dogs because they cannot resist the temptation to chew them. Beanbags are very comforting for young puppies, but be prepared for it to chew it. A plastic basket with a washable blanket is a much better investment. As your dog grows you may need to buy a larger basket.

Larger short-haired breeds may find a basket (with or without a blanket) too hard for them. Their short hair only offers minimal protection for their skin, so they may quickly develop ugly bare patches and callouses. For such breeds, there are a number of purpose-built beds on offer. Ask at your local petshop for the type most suitable for your dog. Put the basket in an out-of-the-way corner, out of draughts. A dog does not like to be separated from the family and likes to know about everything that is happening around him. The most obvious place for the basket, therefore, is the kitchen.

In its land of origin, the Tibetan Terrier is largely used as a shepherd and guard dog

The Keeshond has a luxurious white, golden, black, brown, or wolf-grey coat

A Long-haired Dachshund puppy

Dogs have many retiring areas, and you can expect it to want to be with you while you are awake. Its permanent bed will be used a nighttime. Try to avoid moving its basket around, for it will confuse your dog to find his 'den' missing.

sees the kennel as its 'den'. Make it comfortable with familiar items and perhaps a treat or two. High-quality indoor kennels are often expensive to buy but they are well worth the outlay.

Indoor kennels

If your dog is inclined to be enterprising and to destroy things, or is taking a long time to house-train, an indoor kennel may be the solution. These kennels are appropriate if you plan to go out for short periods, and a healthy dog will not soil its own place. Make sure it

This French Bulldog is enjoying the spring sunshine

Some people believe that indoor kennels are cruel because they limit a dog's freedom of movement. However, a dog who is disciplined and knows that it will receive a warm greeting when it is released from its kennel is bound to be happier than a dog who is consistently told off for being naughty in its owner's absence.

It goes without saying that if you do decide to buy an indoor kennel, it should be introduced as something positive, and never as a form of punishment.

Food and water bowls

Food and water bowls come in all shapes and sizes. Stone-glazed bowls are very beautiful but they have the disadvantage of being relatively expensive and they break when dropped. Plastic bowls are often a good choice as they are easy to clean.

Many good plastic bowls are now guaranteed by the manufacturer. A disadvantage of plastic bowls is that they can be easily chewed. They are also light enough to slide across the floor, which may cause accidents with an over-zealous pet.

Stainless-steel bowls are unbreakable and easy to keep clean. When placed in a holder, they will remain in place on the floor and should

The Jura Laufhund is one of the Swiss hound breeds

Next page: Pembroke Welsh corgis

The big difference between the Norwich terrier (photo) and the Norfolk terrier is that the former has pricked ears and the latter drooping ones

The Spanish Greyhound (Galgo Espanol) is an old Spanish breed which may be short or rough coated

Above left: The Estrela Mountain Dog is an excellent guard dog and pleasant companion

Above: Arctic dogs such as this Alaskan Malamute are comfortable even when temperatures are below freezing

Left: Bi-colour French Bulldog

Right: The collars for greyhounds are wider in the middle than ordinary collars

not slide about. It is better for the posture and digestion of bigger dogs if they are able to eat from a raised platform. Special adjustable feed-bowl holders are available for these animals. Bowls that narrow towards the top are advisable for spaniels and other breeds with long ears to help prevent them from dangling in the food.

These Griffon Bruxellois are playing with a cloth

This dog's mother was a Belgian Shepherd (Malinois). Its father could well have been an Arctic dog

Collars and leads

A collar and lead should be sturdy and well made, especially if you have a very large strong dog. Do not buy a collar big enough for your dog to grow into; it should not be possible to pull it over his head.

Collars and leads are usually made of leather or nylon.
Nylon is often preferable because it is soft, does not damage the dog's coat, and is very strong. An additional advantage is that nylon is washable – a useful feature if you are accustomed to muddy walks.

A metal choke chain should not be used as it will damage the coat. A potentially aggressive dog may require a muzzle when taken out-doors. A longer lead is always more useful than a short one because you can give the dog more freedom of movement.

Retractable leads are also available. These are very useful for daily walks.

When buying collars, chains, and leads, do not just examine the material they are made of: the fastenings, hooks, and rings are equally as important. After all, a chain is only as strong as its weakest link.

Brushes and combs

There are special brushes and combs for every kind of coat. A rubber glove with a bobbly surface is ideal for short-coated dogs: the loose hairs are caught on the rough surface. Long-coated dogs are better groomed with hard brushes and coarse-toothed combs. Flea combs, on the other hand, need to be very fine so that the fleas are caught between the teeth. If you are in any doubt, you could ask your a groomer for advice.

Toys and chewables

Dogs need toys and chewable items, and they are as essential as any other item because your dog will love to play, and to chew on a favourite toy. Chewing encourages healthy gums and teeth and you must make sure that your dog has access to something on which to chew. However, not all the items for sale in a pet shop are necessarily suitable for every dog. In almost all cases it is better to buy a good-quality toy that is recommended by either your breeder or perhaps a dog magazine. Some dogs are very careful with their toys while others can't resist breaking them. Such dogs should not be given plastic or rubber toys, which can be destroyed and perhaps inadvertently eaten.

Some vets and nutritionists believe that a bone is necessary for healthy teeth, but it is unlikely to focus their chewing and you will have to be prepared for your dog to try out its teeth on anything that looks like it might be fun. Over time, it will learn what is acceptable and what is not.

'Bones' made of buffalo hide are available, but your dog will be quite happy with a well boiled beef bone. For the dog's safety, it is better to buy a bigger bone or toy rather than a smaller one.

Young dogs are very playful. This golden Great Dane bitch is almost a year old

TIP

Some grooming is necessary for whatever type of dog you choose and a regular routine should be established when the dog is very young. Try to make these occasions as pleasant as possible. It should be a relaxing and enjoyable experience.

CHAPTER 5

Care

A dog's care is not restricted to exercise and feeding. Depending on the breed, its coat may also need a great deal of looking after. In addition, ears, nails, and teeth will require attention.

Care of the coat

For most dogs, regular grooming will be enough to keep their coats in good condition. Some dogs will also need to have their coats plucked, clipped, or trimmed in one way or another. A few owners consider such trimming to be an unnecessary luxury, but none-

Right: This Great Dane bitch is ten years old, a respectable age for such a large breed

This beautiful Flat-coated Retriever is clearly enjoying all the attention it is being given

theless it is essential. Many rough-coated dogs have coats that need to be pulled, which means pulling the old hairs out by hand so that the new coat can grow through. Exercise caution if you want to do this yourself. It is usually suggested that a professional undertakes this procedure to avoid hurting the dog and setting up unhappy patterns of behaviour.

Pulling a coat is fairly labour-intensive, and done professionally, can be quite expensive. Since clipping has the same visual effect as pulling, but is considerably cheaper, many owners will be tempted to have their dogs clipped instead.

However, when a dog is clipped, its old hairs remain in its coat and these prevent the new coat growing through. This may cause suffocation of its skin, and the dog may begin to suffer from chronic coat and skin problems.

Having your dog's coat pulled professionally two to four times a year is essential to keep him healthy.

Poodles have quite a different kind of coat. Unless this is trimmed or clipped it will simply continue to grow. Poodles need to be brushed and combed several times a week,

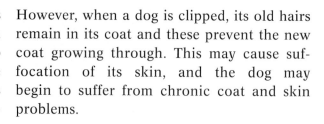

Right: The coat of a Belgian Shepherd Dog (Lakenois) will need regular pulling

The Schnauzer is a rough-coated dog that will need to be trimmed twice a year

Below: Standard Schnauzer

and their coats will need to be clipped by a professional at least five times a year.

Some owners think, wrongly, that breeds such as Golden Retrievers, Irish Setters, and Cocker Spaniels never need to visit a dog parlour. As a consequence, there are many Spaniels, Retrievers, and Setters whose coats are in desperate need of attention. If you are not prepared to have your dog groomed professionally, you must do it yourself.

Other dogs whose coats needing a lot of attention include the Old English Sheepdog, Maltese, the Lhasa Apso, and the Yorkshire Terrier.

Untended, their coats will quickly become so matted that there is no other solution but to shave the dog completely.

Many owners of such dogs therefore occasionally cut their coats short, which considerably simplifies care. All dogs will need to be professionally groomed occasionally, and you should bear that in mind when choosing your pet.

Nail care

Cutting and filing a dog's nails is also part of its normal care. If a dog frequently walks on rough or hard surfaces its nails will wear down naturally.However, this is not the case for all dogs: nails will sometimes continue to grow, and if a dog's nails are too long, its toes will start to spread, and it will develop an unnatural gait. Long nails also break and tear

Affenpinscher

Poodles are generally clipped into a particular style

The coat of an American Cocker Spaniel requires a great deal of care, the ears in particular needing attention

This English Cocker Spaniel is still young but it will soon need to make its first visit to the dog parlour

more easily and can cause considerable pain and discomfort. You should cut your dog's nails with a pair of specially designed nail clippers. If you would rather not cut your dog's nails yourself, a groomer or veterinary surgeon will do it for you.

TIP
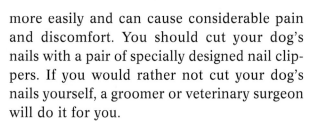
A weekly grooming is never an unnecessary luxury. While brushing the coat you may notice things that you would otherwise have missed, such as small cuts, fleas, and ticks.
In addition, grooming strengthens the bond between the dog and its owner.

Ear care

Your dog's ears will need to be inspected regularly. Excessive hair growth in his ears can cause all sorts of problems, especially if he is long- or rough-coated. Bacteria have every opportunity to breed in the warm moist hollows created by excessive hair growth. These areas will start to itch, and the dog will scratch itself, causing small abrasions which can easily become infected. This will not happen if your dog's ears are inspected at least once a month and any excess hair removed.

Even short-coated dogs, especially those breeds with long ears such as Bassets and Spaniels, need to have their ears looked after carefully. With a good ear cleaner you can keep his ears clean yourself.

Don't use cotton wool buds since these generally just push the dirt further into the ear.

Treatment for fleas

Parasites such as fleas are very difficult to eradicate. They are very hardy, and in mild weather breed at a tremendous rate.

Flea problems are worse in summer when the weather is warm and humid. Even if your dog appears not to have fleas, it does not necessarily mean that there are no fleas in your house. By far the largest number of fleas live in your home, not on the dog itself. Research as shown that a flea's eggs can hatch after several years of dormancy. So an anti-flea campaign will only work if you treat your dog and his environment. Vacuum often, especially in corners and crevices – paying particular attention to soft upholstery. Wash your dog's blankets frequently.

Use a good flea powder to treat rugs, carpets, and your dog's basket. There are numerous anti-flea substances on the market, some of which work rather better than others. There are specially designed products that are 'environmentally friendly'. Take care not to use products designed for furniture or clothing on your dog.

When in doubt, ask your veterinary surgeon for advice.

Lhasa Apso

Soft-coated Wheaten Terrier puppies have a quite different coat from the adult dog

Removing ticks

Ticks are parasites that feed on the blood of their host. Your dog will normally pick these up in fields where sheep or other animals graze. It is only after they have penetrated your dog's skin with their heads and powerful jaws and have filled themselves with your dog's blood that they will become visible as grey bobbles.

If you just simply pull the tic out its head may remain under your dog's skin, and this can cause all kinds of infections.

If you place a piece of cotton wool soaked in alcohol on the tick it will lose its grip. You can then pull it out gently, slowly twisting it as you do so.

Australian Silky Terriers have no undercoat and rarely moult

Wire-haired Fox Terrier. Fox Terriers can be smooth or wire haired

Above: Labrador Retriever

Left: An older dog, such as this English Cocker Spaniel, needs additional care and attention

Below: This mongrel's coat is in excellent condition

Care of the teeth

Teeth are as important to a dog than they are to humans. Like us, dogs use their teeth to eat and to chew but they are also a form of defence. A dog also uses its teeth to fetch and carry sticks and balls. You can keep your dog's teeth healthy by providing him regularly with things to chew. Chewing helps to scrape the teeth and thereby prevents plaque from forming. Regular chewing will help to keep his teeth and gums healthy. Chewable toys should be available at all times, and not just as a treat.

Some nutritionists believe that you should not give your dog rabbit or poultry bones because they can splinter and become lodged in the digestive tract. A good canine toothbrush and toothpaste, available from your local pet shop, should also be used on a daily basis to keep your dog's mouth and teeth clean.
Heavy tartar should be removed by a profes-

sional – don't be tempted to scrape at it yourself, for you will likely cause damage to the gums. Dogs, just like people, suffer a great deal of pain when their teeth rot. Bad teeth can also give them very bad breath. If your dog's teeth begin to rot, it will eventually be unable to eat solid food, so take steps to prevent tooth decay before it sets in.

Feeding

It is best to divide your dog's daily ration into two meals. It is better for his digestion to spread the amount of food he eats over the day. There are many different kinds of dog food and so every owner needs to decide what is most suitable for their own dog.

A dog's faeces should be firm, its coat should shine, and its overall appearance should be that of general health. If this is not the case, it could be that your dog is eating the wrong kind of food, or it could be that he is simply feeling under the weather.

Some dogs have an allergic reaction to the colouring, preservatives, or certain types of protein in dog food. If you are not entirely happy with your dog's diet, you should consult your veterinary surgeon.

Many people choose a 'complete food', which means that all of the elements of nutrition necessary to keep your dog healthy will be contained in a single food. You won't need to add any extra vitamins or minerals to his diet, which simplifies the feeding process. Other foods need to be mixed with complementary feed. Obviously the size and the age of your dog will dictate its nutritional requirements and you will need to calculate your dog's ideal calorie intake. While most dogs will eat a wide range of foodstuffs similar to those contained in a human diet, including meat, vegetables, cereals and even fresh fruit, puppies need careful feeding up until the age of about seven

The coats of the Basset Bleu de Gascogne need little care, but their long ears require additional attention

St Bernard

months. Avoid giving your dog confectionery and other sweet snacks. Nutritious chews and biscuits are available as treats and rewards. A good supply of fresh drinking water should always be available, and if your dog is new to your family, give it bottled water until it has had time to adjust to the tap water in your area.

Make sure your dog does not become overweight. Fat dogs are not only less active, but they may also suffer from back and heart problems, and have a much shorter life expectancy. A good rule of thumb is that a dog's ribs should be easy to feel. If you have to press hard, your dog is too fat.

Inoculations

A dog needs to be inoculated and wormed regularly. Your veterinary surgeon will give you an inoculation and worming plan, which you must be certain to follow carefully.

Worms can have a devastating effect on a dog's intestines, many of the diseases inoculated against in the UK can prove fatal. There is no reason why you should run this risk. Rabies inoculations are not compulsory in all countries, but if you take your dog abroad you will usually need to show a valid inoculation certificate at the border. In the UK this is a tremendously complicated procedure undertaken through the Ministry of Agriculture and it will be necessary to put your dog into quarantine for six months upon your return to the country.

Care of the older dog

The average life expectancy of a dog is ten to fourteen years. Large dogs will generally age sooner than smaller ones. Most dogs age almost imperceptibly – others, like Great Danes and Wolfhounds can go from adulthood at five to senility at six or seven, and then die.

As it ages, your dog will not be so playful and his reactions will slow down. Ageing can also be accompanied by certain problems. As many older dogs have trouble with their digestion, it is better to give them a diet that is lower in protein. There are special foods available for older dogs and your vet will advise you of the one most suitable for your dog.

An older dog's hearing will be less acute and it may develop cataracts that can hinder its sight. Getting out of its basket will become

Borzoi

Golden Retriever

more difficult and the dog may have painful joints. It is therefore better to give older dogs a soft bed. Some older dogs become irritable and short-tempered – partly because they are frustrated by the physical effects of ageing, and partly because they may begin to feel insecure when their strength is fading. They may begin to howl when the family is out even if they have never done so before. There is one thing you must never forget. Your dog gave you the best years of his life. Now that he is getting older, he needs you more than ever before. Do not let him down. If he develops an illness which causes him pain and discomfort, or which is incurable, you should not let him suffer unnecessarily. However difficult it may be, your dog will be better off if you put him to sleep when this is necessary rather than extending his life by a few painful and fear-filled months.

If you have children it is wise to involve them in this decision. You must try to explain to them that dying is something that is a part of life. We must accept this very unpleasant responsibility as part and parcel of accepting a dog into our lives.

TIP

Every coat is different. A comb or brush suitable for a long-coated dog may not be effective for a short- or wire-coated dog. For wire-coated dogs, a medium-toothed metal comb is very helpful. The dead undercoat can be removed even more quickly using a comb with two rows of teeth.

TIP

It is good practice to remove excessive hair growth between the pads of the feet regularly. Use a curved pair of scissors with blunt ends. If the curved side of the scissors is held towards the pads, you will not cut the foot accidentally.

CHAPTER 6

Canine behaviour

Always study your dog's body language. Mutual understanding can only be achieved between you and your dog if you understand his body language.

Right: Basset Artésian Normands are friendly, gentle dogs who like company

Chihuahua

The behaviour of wolves

As discussed in Chapter One, the most likely ancestor of the domestic dog is the wolf. Wolves live in small packs, each of which has a leader. The pack leader is responsible for seeing to all of the she-wolves in the pack as they come in season, and for leading the entire pack. All the other pack members have their own particular place in the pack's hierarchy.

The wolves regularly confirm their positions within the pack by means of signals. This ensures there is no confusion about roles so fights are minimised. Fighting could reduce the pack numbers and wolves need each

By crouching down and holding his ears pressed backwards, this small Basset Griffon Vendeen puppy is making it quite clear that the Rottweiler has the higher status

other to survive, not least because they hunt as a pack. Fights to the death usually only occur when the pack leader begins to lose his strength. A weak pack leader puts the survival of the pack at risk and so will eventually be killed or driven away by a stronger or younger wolf, before a new leader takes its place. High-ranking wolves enjoy certain privileges the lower-ranking wolves do not enjoy.

In most cases high-ranking wolves are the first to eat prey and the first to be greeted by the pack leader. A lower-ranking wolf is subservient to those of a higher rank. Although many of the wild, survival-orientated instincts of the dog have been suppressed through domestication, most dogs retain a territorial and predatory instinct to a varying degree. Natural pack behaviour will lead your dog to protect the home, which it considers the pack's communal den, against undesirable

There is no need for an in-depth behavioural study to understand what this Pekinese wants to express by his imploring look

intruders. In most instances, a dog will look to its human owner, the pack leader, for instruction on how to behave towards a stranger.

Body language

Your dog sees the family of which he is a part as his pack. Since he cannot talk to us he establishes his rank within the family by means of his behaviour. Dogs within a family are not usually concerned with their 'rank';

they are all subordinate and view their owners as something between a pack leader and a parental figure, not a survival competitor.

Your dog will feel the need to respond to your commands, so make sure you do so fairly and consistently.

Correct him if he behaves inappropriately A dog may display aggression in many different circumstances – for example, it its own defence, or to impose its will on other dogs or people. Sometimes it may be necessary to call in the assistance of a professional dog trainer to help in the education of a dominant dog.

A submissive is easy to recognise because in a confrontation with humans or with another dog, it will lower its head or tail. When you stroke it, it will lower its body and fold his ears backwards. Lower-ranking dogs frequently lick higher-ranking dogs under their chins. If a dog does this to us he is showing us that we have nothing to fear from it and that it is solicitous.

If your dog regularly displays very shy or submissive behaviour you should to improve his self-confidence. A behaviour therapist will know several ways of doing this. It is not possible to teach a dog to respond to commands to increase self-confidence in a range of social situations but a professional behaviour therapist will be able to change habits gently and improve self-esteem according to your dog's individual needs.

These types of canine behaviour are all easily recognisable. There are of course many different patterns of behaviour between the obviously dominant or aggressive dog and the one that is underconfident and submissive dog. For example, a dog may show his teeth and growl dangerously even though his whole posture suggests a subservient position. Its

This young Belgian Shepherd (Malinois) is inviting the Cesky Terrier to play

The attentive gaze of the Vizsla (Hungarian Vizsla)

tail will be between its legs, its ears flat back against its neck, and it will have made its body as small as possible. A dog behaving in this way is showing defensive aggression, which is a feature of his survival instinct. Your dog probably feels threatened, and it is best to find ways to communicate that it has nothing to fear.

If you are planning to acquire a second dog, you will need to consider one or two important things. Dogs and bitches generally get along very well, but two dogs or two bitches can make each other miserable. Most male and female dogs get along well, although it will depend on the individual characters of the dogs to some degree. Male and female dogs will not usually fight – certainly not for 'leadership', but you may encounter other problems that can be deal with by a behaviour therapist or an experienced veterinary surgeon.

There are numerous books devoted to the discussion of behaviour and it is a good idea to familiarise yourself with the meaning of your dog's body language instead of trying to 'train' it to behave differently. Increasing your understanding of your dog's body language can only improve your relationship with him.

Signals to other dogs

Some dogs have a very well-developed sense of smell. Dogs communicate with body language and verbally, and also use their sense of smell. A dog's nose is moist in order to help it to capture scent. Scents carried in the nasal

Below: The powerful and watchful Dogue de Bordeaux makes an excellent bodyguard

Right: The Japanese Akita is clearly the more dominant of the two dogs. The other shows his acceptance of his subordinate position by his lower body and by the position of his ears.

Above: Havanese

Left: A young Bull Mastiff

Below: Alaskan Malamute

secretions are passed to the nasal membranes which are lined with sensory cells leading directly to the olfactory bulb of the brain. The region of a dog's brain which registers smell has about 40 times more cells than the equivalent area in a human brain.

Dogs are able to ascertain from the smell of urine or faeces, and the places where these smells occur, the condition of the dog that made these smells. Some experts believe that they are able to tell from these scents whether, for example, the dog is new to the area, whether it is ill, or is a bitch in season. When they have decided what the scent means, they may leave a message behind for other dogs in their urine and by scratching the ground with their nails. Although there is no need to let your dog extend its walk excessively by sniffing around everywhere, it is unkind to stop him from sniffing completely. A dog's daily walk round the block is the canine equivalent of reading a newspaper.

A dog's hearing is also much sharper than man's and their ears are more mobile. They can detect high-frequency sounds inaudible to humans and have a greater sensitivity to sound than we do. Research has shown that a dog can pinpoint the source of a sound within six-hundredths of a second.

The position of the eyes on a dog's head give it a wider field of vision than humans'. Unless the eyes are situated at the front of the head the animal will tend to have poor stereoscopic vision and less ability to judge distance. Dogs have better eyesight in low light levels and are more sensitive to light than humans.

Dogs and cats

If dogs and cats can get to know each other when they are both young, they will learn to understand each other's body language. Not infrequently, dogs and cats can become life-long friends.

Older pets may have trouble adjusting to a new family member, so bear that in mind when considering a new pet.

Dogs learn a lot about each other from the scent of their urine

A German Long-haired Pointer and a Belgian Shepherd Dog (Groenendael)

CHAPTER 7

Sporting dogs

Sporting dogs form the largest single group of pedigree dogs. This is hardly surprising as most dogs were originally bred to help humans in the hunt.

Some breeds are highly specialised.

Rechts: Beagles worden veel voor de hazenjacht gebruikt

The flesh-coloured stripe between the nostrils of the German Hound (Deutsche Bracke) is an essential characteristic of this breed

Basset Hound

The Labrador Retriever is still frequently used as a hunting dog

Hounds

Hounds usually hunt in packs and have very well developed noses which they can rely on for hunting. When they are released on to the field, they spread out until one of them picks up the scent. This dog announces his find loudly so that the others can join him. This 'giving voice' is very important for the hunters; it helps them tell exactly where the pack is, even from a considerable distance. Such hunts can take many hours, so the dogs need to be in excellent condition. Although it looks as though all the dogs are following the scent, in fact it is just one. This hound shows the rest of the pack the route to follow. It would be too much for one dog to be solely responsible for discriminating between the

The Labrador Retriever is still frequently used as a hunting dog

A standard Basset Griffon Vendéen

The Pointer has been bred to seek out partridges

this kind of dog has been bred selectively for hunting and will have the specific characteristics of a hunting dog to a greater or lesser degree. Hounds are naturally tolerant of other dogs and are keen hunters.

Dogs don't usually like being on their own. They are happiest with the companionship of another dog – particularly another hound, since the group is accustomed to living and hunting in great packs – or humans. A hound that must spend his days alone in his kennel will loudly announce his displeasure to his surroundings. The independence necessary for hounds in the field can mean that, as a family dog, they are somewhat less responsive to training than other breeds, although patient instruction can do a great deal to overcome this.

scent and other traces that it continually encounters during the hunt, and so the dogs take turns. A hound can make a very good family dog so long as its owner recognises that

English Setters

Flat-Coated Retriever

All hounds are passionate about hunting, which makes it difficult for them to ignore an interesting scent. Hounds must therefore never be allowed to run loose in an area where there is a lot of game, since their instinctive need for hunting could well overcome their bonding with their owner. Hounds are generally very kind, gentle, and affectionate dogs.

They are usually good with children and greet visitors with great enthusiasm.

The Chesapeake Bay Retriever has an unusual, slightly oily coat, evolved to protect it in the water

Well-known hounds include the Bloodhound, the Beagle, and the various Bassets. Less well-known hounds include Pharoah and the Otter Hound.

Setters, Pointers and Retrievers

Sporting dogs with quite a different family background are the Setters, Pointers, and Retrievers. These breeds principally originated in the British Isles and North America and are occasionally used together by hunters.

Setters and Pointers are good at drawing attention to the whereabouts of game. After being instructed to do so by the hunter, they will can be trained to comb the area indicated for wildfowl. When they have located the

The Wetterhoun, also known as the Friesian Curly Coated Hound, was used as a retriever but also functioned as a guard dog

game, they stand immobile, their noses pointing in the direction of the prey. Frequently they will also lift one of their front legs and hold their tail straight out behind them. In this way, the hunter can see exactly where the game is. Setters and Pointers aren't very good retrievers as they have not been bred to do this. Hunters therefore usually also take a Retriever with them to collect the game.

Retrievers are also frequently used to retrieve waterfowl. Almost without exception, they love swimming. Hunters set great store by the so-called 'soft mouth' of their Retrievers. This means that the dog carries the game so carefully when retrieving it that the game is not damaged.

Pointers and Setters, such as the English, Irish, and Gordon Setter, as well as Retrievers, such as the Golden, Labrador, and Flat-coated Retriever, are good, loyal, and gentle family dogs. They all require a great deal of exercise and lots of contact with their owner or handler. Retriever breeds are among some of the most obedient of dogs, while Setters tend to be more independently minded.

Chesapeake Bay Retrievers, together with Curly-coated Retrievers, are the only two Retriever breeds that were bred not only for hunting but also to guard and defend their homes and owners. Consequently their characters are somewhat tougher and their training is a little more difficult.

Above: The German Short-haired Pointer is an active and obedient hunting dog

Centre: The German Rough-Haired Pointer is a good, hardworking, all-round hunting dog

Below: The Cesky Fousek is an all-round hunting dog

Right: This Auvergne Pointer, the Braque D'Auvergne, is used to hunt game birds

Epagneul Français

Centre: The Italian Spinone is an all-round hunting dog, with considerable powers of endurance. They are either white, or white with brown or orange markings. They are gentle and friendly dogs with a remarkable scenting ability

Below left: The Borzoi was originally bred to hunt wolves

Below: Whippets

Right: The Hungarian Vizsla is a hunting dog that can be either short- or rough-coated. It is used not only as a pointer and retriever, but also to follow a scent

The Ibizan Hound hunts using not only his nose and hearing but also his sight

The Airedale Terrier can be stubborn and aloof

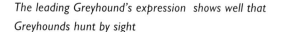

The leading Greyhound's expression shows well that Greyhounds hunt by sight

All-round hunting dogs

In continental Europe most hunting dogs are all-rounders: they not only show the game but also retrieve it. Examples of such hunting dogs are German Pointers, the Czechoslovakian Pointer (Cesky Fousek), and the Epagneul Français. Most Spaniels are hunting dogs that are usually employed to flush out and retrieve feathered game.

The various all-round hunting dogs, as well as the Spaniels, generally make first-class family dogs, because they are usually able to adjust to being a household pet as long as they get enough exercise. Some hunting dogs are prone to behaviour problems, and Spaniels in particular may not find it easy to adjust to life

Cairn Terriers were once used to hunt underground vermin   *Scottish Terrier*

as a non-working companion. Most of these problems can be ironed out over time.

Greyhounds

Greyhounds are the oldest hunting dogs known. They are different from all other hunting dogs in that they hunt entirely by sight. For this reason dogs like this are also

known as 'sight hounds' Greyhounds locate, chase, and kill their quarry entirely on their own, without the help of other dogs or commands from their handler.

These thoroughbreds can attain enormous speeds. When chasing their quarry focus on it to such a degree that all else is forgotten. It is for this reason that some countries have banned hunting with these dogs. In heavily populated areas with many roads they can

The Irish Wolfhound, like the Borzoi, was bred to hunt wolves   *Argentinian Mastiff (Dogue d'Argentine)*   *The Elkhound has been bred to hunt elk*

The speciality of the Finnish Spitz is hunting the auerhoen

English Bulldog

West Siberian Laika

pose a danger not only to themselves but also to road users if they are not kept on a lead.

When Greyhounds are kept as household pets they are very affectionate, gentle and even sensitive dogs that are very good with children. They rarely have problems with other dogs.
When they get enough exercise, they are very quiet in the house, even lazy. They usually live very happily with other animals that they recognise as part of their 'group', but their

hunting instinct poses a threat to other people's cats, small dogs or rabbits. Some examples of Greyhound breeds are the Greyhound, Whippet, and the Irish Wolfhound. Over the hundreds and, in some cases, thousands of years that these dogs have accompanied humans, some curious legends have arisen about them. One of the most remarkable of these is set in Ireland. According to this legend, Prince Llewelyn left his wolfhound Gelert guarding his young son while he goes hunting. On his return, Llewelyn finds the tent

Dachshund, also known as Teckel

This Dutch Partridge Dog (Drentse Patrijshond) is trained first to retrieve a dummy

in a terrible state; everything is covered with blood and the baby is nowhere to be seen. Gelert, his muzzle covered in blood, lies in a corner eyeing his owner anxiously.

Llewelyn concludes that the dog must have attacked the child and, in fury, he kills the dog with his spear.

Only later does he find the corpse of a huge wolf and sees his son sleeping unharmed under his cradle. The courage and loyalty shown by Gelert cost him his life.

Deeply saddened, Llewelyn buries his loyal friend in a valley. This valley is still called 'Bedd Gelert' in Ireland, in memory of this loyal dog.

Terriers

Terriers are a separate group of hunting dogs. Just like Greyhounds, they are fairly independent and can be trained to hunt well. They are tremendously courageous and enthusiastic hunters.

The word Terrier comes from 'terra' meaning earth: terriers are sometimes called 'earth dogs'. They can be divided into long-legged (normal) and short-legged breeds.

The short-legged Terriers had the advantage when hunting foxes and rabbits because they could chase them into the ground. They were also frequently used to exterminate vermin such as rats. Some long-legged Terriers, such as the Manchester Terrier, proved to be excellent ratters.

In England, contests were once organised in which Manchester Terriers had to kill as many rats as possible within a certain time limit in specially created arenas. Such events attracted enormous crowds and the winners were treated with great respect.

Dutch Partridge Dogs

The Jamthund is still used in Scandinavia to hunt elk

Although today Terriers are usually kept as pets, their true nature has not altered dramatically. They are sharp, lively, and extrovert dogs with pronounced characters.

Specialist dogs

Alongside the many Terriers, Greyhounds, Retrievers, Hounds, and Setters, other dogs have also been bred for specialised forms of hunting. For example, in Scandinavia there are a number of breeds, including the Elk Hound and the Jamthund, which are specialised elkhunters. Their job is to locate the elk and, by barking loudly, to keep it where it is until the hunter arrives to shoot it.

Bearing in mind the size and strength of their quarry, these dogs need to be very courageous.

Another Scandinavian breed, the Finnish Spitz, is used to hunt a variety of game, such as bears and rabbits. However, it is an expert in locating and flushing out the 'auerhoen' – a local bird. This skill has given these delightful household pets the nickname 'barking bird-hound'.

There is a similar specialist hound in Africa called the Rhodesian Ridgeback. The name refers to the ridge of hair on the dog's back, which grows in the opposite direction to the rest of his coat. Rhodesian Ridgebacks are used as lion hunters in their natural environment, but are also very good family dogs.

In Argentina, a breed has been developed to hunt pumas and wild boar by crossing local dogs with Great Danes and Bull Terriers. These courageous and very powerful dogs, known as Argentinian Mastiffs (Dogue d'Argentine), are very keen hunters.

Pros and cons of hunting

Some countries have stronger traditions of hunting than others, and most countries also have very strict rules about how it should be done.

In many countries, hunters need a licence and the hunting of certain kinds of game is restricted to particular times of year. In these countries public opinion is often particularly fierce against hunting. Opponents of hunting argue, among other things, that many animals have a hard enough time to survive without being hunted by humans. They claim that hunters are far less selective than they purport to be. Hunt supporters argue that selective hunting has a positive effect on the animal population, drawing on the laws of nature to

support them. In areas of the world where wolves and feline predators occur in sufficient numbers, weak and sickly animals have little chance to multiply. In this way the breed remains strong and healthy.

The laws of nature are hard but justifiable; where there are few predators, many animals will die of hunger because there is too little food. Only the strongest will be able to survive hard times.

Laws ensure that the populations of these different kinds of animals are kept in balance; no single species has the chance to multiply faster than any other, and the disastrous consequences of such a situation are therefore avoided. Where rabbits, hares and pheasants no longer have any natural predators, Man, the hunter, must intervene to keep the natural balance. There is, of course, some argument

A German Long-Haired Pointer

The Rhodesian Ridgeback is an African dog that was bred to hunt lions

that a 'natural' balance can not really exist because all environments where men go are 'managed'.

Both hunters and environmentalists have elements of their arguments that carry weight. It is true that a wild animal can live a normal, natural life before being killed, while the vast numbers of animals kept for human consumption, such as pigs, calves, and chickens have precious little time to to enjoy before they are fattened, transported and subsequently slaughtered.

Animal-friendly forms of hunting
It is useful for the opponents of hunting to know that there a number of types of hunting and hunting competitions which do not kill animals. For example, special hunting competitions have been developed for Dachshunds to test their skill and courage in hunting foxes. A tame, specially trained fox is used and during the test, no blood flows. The Dachshund sees it as very exciting and serious, whereas the fox, judging by his reaction, sees the whole thing as an interesting interlude. At the end, the fox simply goes home with one of the hunters.

An artificial scent is also frequently used for hunting with hounds and hunting tests for retrievers sometimes use dummies. In these forms of hunting no game is shot.

CHAPTER 8

Shepherds and sheepdogs

Although sheepdogs are rarely used today for the original purpose of herding sheep, there are still many breeds with broadly the same characteristics as their ancestors for.

Right: The Schapendoes is a Dutch breed

The Beauceron (Berger de Beauce), also known as the Bas Rouge (red sock)

German Shepherd Dog

Border Collie

Guarding and herding dogs

Many centuries ago dogs were used all over the world as sheepdogs. There was no facility for irrigating the land in times of drought and the landscape was not crossed by motorways packed with fast-moving cars. Herds could move undisturbed from one place to another. If there was enough to eat, the herd remained in the same place until drought made it necessary to move on to more fertile land. The herd was accompanied by a shepherd who kept a sharp eye on the condition of the animals. Every now and then some animals would be sold at market or the sheep would be sheared for their thick wool. It was also sometimes necessary to separate some animals from the rest because they had been sold or because they were injured and required special attention. In some parts of the world these conditions exist today.

In this situation a good sheepdog was and still is invaluable. These special dogs need to have a very close relationship with the shepherd in order to understand all the signs he gives them and to be able to act upon them. Shepherd and dogs have always worked together as a well-rehearsed team.

Below left: The Bearded Collie is a friendly, outgoing, and gentle shepherd dog

Below: A Border Collie at work with a sheep

The tips of Shetland Sheepdogs' ears drop forward

Pembroke Welsh Corgi

It is therefore not surprising that this type of dog has produced breeds that combine considerable focus with a tremendous will to work. This large group of hard-working dogs includes, among others, the Border Collie, the Sheltie, the Old English Sheepdog and the Cardigan Welsh and Pembroke Welsh Corgis. Although the Rottweiler was also used as a

The Cardigan Welsh Corgi is a little larger than the Pembroke Welsh Corgi

Cardigan Welsh Corgi

A Rotweiller is a very protective dog

herding dog, it has less of the true sheepdog character. This can be explained by looking at the history of its development. The Rottweiler comes from the German town of Rottweil, where it was principally kept by butchers and cattle dealers. When animals needed to be driven to the city for sale or slaughter, the Rottweiler functioned as a herd dog. On the way back home, the dog's owner frequently carried a great deal of money. The Rottweiler then acted as a very convincing personal bodyguard. Today the Rottweiler is more a guard dog than a herding dog.

Herd guard dogs

In addition to dogs to herd the animals, shepherds sometimes also needed a dog to guard

Entlebuch Mountain Dogs (Entlebucher Sennenhund) were used as guard and hauling dogs and also to herd cattle

Above: The coat of the Old English Sheepdog needs a lot of care

Above right: The Australian Cattle dog is a superb herding dog

Below right: Dalmatian

the herd against two- and four-footed robbers. Usually a different dog was employed for this since most herding dogs were slim, athletic, medium-sized dogs who could offer little defence against sheep rustlers or predators. Obedience was not a necessity; a good guard dog worked alone and needed neither commands nor signs from the shepherd to spring into action. Herd guard dogs were generally fairly large and strong, and in colder areas had a thick coat which not only protected them against the cold but also against the attacks of wolves or large felines.

Guarding dogs view sheep and other livestock as parental figures, and so stay with them, follow them and don't attack them as prey. They are very 'juvenile' in nature compared with the new 'predator' of the herding dogs.

Herd guard dogs include breeds such as the Komondor and the Maremma Sheepdog. The Komondor has an unusual coat, which probably makes him the most remarkable of the herd guard dogs. His coat has a pronounced tendency to mat and, over time, it forms long panels or cords. This provides the dog with an impenetrably thick blanket that protects him not only from extreme weather conditions but also forms a natural defence against predators.

A Maremma Sheepdog

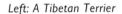

Left: A Tibetan Terrier

Below: A young Spanish Mastiff (Mastin Espagnol)

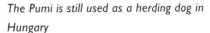

The Pumi is still used as a herding dog in Hungary

If such a dog is kept as a household pet, his owner will from time to time need to separate out the large mats to create cords of uniform thickness.

In the past, the Komondor could only be given a bath in the summer as it could take days to dry out his coat. Today, hairdryers and centrally heated rooms can speed up the process.

Herd guard dogs are generally excellent guard dogs with strong characters. They all need a great deal of space and generally prefer fresh air to a cosy spot by the fireside.

Working sheepdogs

These days there are not many sheepdog breeds which are still used for their original purpose, but alternative occupations have been found for some of these willing, active breeds in order to satisfy their desire to work.

At many outdoor events, Border Collies are invited to exhibit their skills with sheep. Especially in the British Isles, these dogs are regularly tested at sheepdog trials. These dogs are still trained as working dogs, and are able to exhibit their skills in an artificial environment. In Australia a number of cattle-herding dogs, such as the Australian Cattle Dog, are still used for their original purpose.

The Hungarian Puli has an unusual coat

Briards used to guard the flocks in France against four- and two-footed marauders

In Australia, herds are often left to their own devices for long periods of time. When the time comes to sell some of the animals, modern shepherds locate their herds with, among other things, the help of helicopters.

At this point the sheepdogs are brought in to gather the animals together. A good sheepdog is invaluable and many are specifically trained for the vast, rugged landscape.

It is said that in Hungary you can also see some native breeds, such as the Pumi and Puli, working with herds. Breeds such as the Maremma Sheepdog guard the herds that wander in the mountains just as they have for centuries. Indeed, throughout most of the world working dogs are an important part of country living and are trained for their individual and necessary skills. Because of their naturally strong protective instincts, they are also used, as they have for centuries, to protect the homestead and today that role is extended to cover factories and other industrial premises. Some modern dogs, such as the Dobermann, were specifically bred as securi-ty dogs, but other formidable guard dogs tend to come from the herding and allied breeds.

CHAPTER 9

Canine sports

Many working dogs no longer fulfil their original functions. However, because both dogs and owners enjoy it, all sorts of alternatives have been devised so that owners and their dogs can still work together.

Right: German Shepherd in action in an agility test

The Papillon is a small, intelligent companion dog that is good in agility competitions

Natural desire for work

These days, few dogs still perform the tasks they were originally bred to do.

For example, the gun has replaced the swift-footed Greyhound; barbed wire and wooden fencing keep flocks of sheep and herds of cattle on many farmers' land; and snowmobiles have rendered sledge dogs obsolete in many polar regions.

This Alaskan Malamute shows that, with proper guidance, he is capable of extraordinary feats

Although still used for their original purposes in some parts of the world, working dogs are now less essential to day-to-day living in the Western world. Most breeds have adapted to new circumstances, but there are still breeds that are difficult to keep as family pets.

These dogs have such a deeply rooted instinct to work that they are unable to change. To keep these dogs happy, sports have been developed as an alternative to work.

Through the tunnel

Agility

Agility and fly-ball are canine sports that are fast gaining popularity. Agility trials require the dog to negotiate a course of obstacles as faultlessly as possible.

As well as ordinary obstacles like those used in equine showjumping, there are fixed elements like the slalom used to challenge working dogs.

Many dog clubs have built their own agility courses, and members train their dogs enthusiastically for national and international competitions. In principle, all breeds can enter agility competitions, as long as both the dog and his owner enjoy it. Different courses are designed to suit different sizes of dog.

Sheepdog breeds such as the Border Collie and the Sheltie generally do very well in com-

This Borzoi looks as though he's enjoying himself

Border Collies are usually quick learners

petitions. Considering their background, these dogs have the best mentality for this kind of sport: they need a lot of contact with their owners and, because of their intelligence, quick reactions, and desire to work, they can be trained to perform well.

Other breeds that are naturally more independent – and generally more difficult to train – are occasionally entered for competitions. These dogs' achievements only go to prove their owner's efforts in training them and the excellent contact that the owner has been able to build up with his dog.

Part of an agility test

Fly-ball

Fly-ball

This Belgian Shepherd Dog (Tervueren) does very well in agility and fly-ball classes. He also shines in obedience trials

Fly-ball

Fly-ball is a team sport for dogs and their owners in which the dogs have to negotiate a row of simple obstacles.

At the end of the obstacles is a machine that throws out a ball when the dog pushes a handle. The dog must catch this ball and return it to his owner via the same line of obstacles.

As soon as the first dog returns, the next may be sent down the line.

The team is therefore very dependent on one another. If one dog runs past an obstacle or has problems with the ball, this can present problems for the whole team.

Just as in agility competitions, the various sheepdog breeds do particularly well at fly-ball.

Greyhound racing

Greyhound racing is a very old sport, reserved exclusively for Greyhound breeds, such as the Whippet, the Greyhound, and the Afghan Hound. Greyhounds are also known as 'sight hounds' because they rely principally on their very sharp sight when chasing their prey. This contrasts to many other breeds, which rely on their superb scenting ability to locate their prey.

Greyhounds are built for speed and naturally chase after fast-moving objects. Since greyhounds are prohibited from hunting in many countries, the racetrack is the only place where these dogs can use up their boundless energy. While racing, the dogs wear muzzles to prevent them hurting each other in the heat of the moment.

The prey' is a projectile – usually an artificial 'rabbit' that travels at great speed along a rail in front of the dogs. It travels just a little faster than the fastest dog because the dogs are not intended actually to catch the 'prey' before they pass the finish. Greyhounds can run at enormous speeds. A well-trained Greyhound can easily sprint at a speed of 65 km ph.

Only dogs in perfect condition are allowed to enter these races to avoid injury to those who are not in good health.

Sledge dogs

In the past, a sledge with a team of Arctic dogs was the only fast and reliable means of transport Eskimos and other natives.

Huskies, Greenland Dogs (Gronlandshund), and Alaskan Malamutes were all greatly prized for their skills. For many years these valuable dogs were scarcely ever exported to other countries. With the development of the snowmobile and other motorised forms of transport, Arctic dogs in many places became unemployed from one day to the next. Nevertheless, the different breeds of Arctic dog have often been preserved for posterity.

They are powerful dogs, well suited to living and working in bitter polar regions because of their build and coat, as well as their mentality.
It is not surprising that most Arctic dogs have difficulty in adapting to life as household pets.

Iceland Dog bitch with her puppies

Pyrenean Sheepdogs perform well in agility and fly-ball competitions

Greyhounds at the start

Greyhounds at the off

A Greyhound race

Sledge-dog competitions

Fortunately, these dogs have a chance to re-live former times by entering competition, and owners of sledge dogs in temperate countries regularly travel to colder places to take part in such events. There are also 'trolley' races on footpaths in forests, rather than sledge races on snow or ice.

Just like Greyhounds, however, Arctic dogs must be very well trained before they can enter. In the absence of snow, they are har-nessed to 'exercise cart' to improve their condition and learn the considerable skills involved. In many countries it is against the law to harness dogs to carts or sledges be-cause of possible injury.

Arctic dogs are, however, an exception, and you can give them no greater pleasure than

letting them pull a sledge. Siberian Huskies, lighter built than the other sledge-dog breeds, are by far the fastest.

Attack dog training

Some people believe that attack dog training makes dogs more aggressive. However, this is not actually the case: dangerously aggressive dogs are those dogs which display unpredicta-ble aggressive behaviour. They behave extre-mely fiercely in situations that should not normally invite a dog's aggression.

Fortunately, you do not often come across dangerously unreliable dogs. This type of training is mainly to harness aggression into a predictable behaviour pattern. Rigorous training is essential. Many countries object to this type of training on the grounds that it is both dangerous and an unsuitable encouragement of aggression in domestic animals.

The idea is that attack training teaches a dog to bite people, but only at his handler's command and not otherwise. Assistants specially trained in man work play the part of a criminal who has to be caught. The dogs are trained only to bite into the sleeve but, since dogs too can make mistakes, the assistant wears a body-suit to protect himself against over-enthusiastic pupils.
Great discipline is required from the dog's handler as well as from the dog.

Both handler and dog need to work as a team, trusting and understanding each other completely. The dog must always obey its handler; independent action is not appreciated. It goes without saying that obedience training is an essential part of all attack training such as man work. A dog trained correctly for man work has to be more reliable than any other dog.

Some dogs are trained to become police dogs and end up working for the police or the army after passing a course of training. These dogs

Arctic dogs

more than earn their keep in dangerous situations, and a good police dog will help maintain order. In some countries dogs are trained in this way purely as a hobby, with a variety of different diplomas and certificates that a dog can earn, and there are also national and international competitions. The dogs most frequently used in this type of training are the German, Belgian, and Dutch Shepherds, Rottweilers, Bouviers, and Dobermanns.

Working Dogs
Even though dogs are used increasingly less as working animals, there still remain certain jobs that can only be done by well-trained dogs.

One has only to think of the many dogs used to help the blind, to assist in avalanche and other rescue teams, and to follow the scents of humans, drugs, animals or anything else. There is no piece of machinery or method of communication that could take over the work of these dogs.

A potential guide dog needs to prove that he is suitable for this kind of work. If he is too easily distracted by other dogs or people he is not capable of taking responsibility for a visually handicapped person.

All these hard-working dogs have, through the ages, been an irreplaceable asset to humanity and require very special training.

CHAPTER 10

Showing

The very first dog show was organised in Belgium in 1847. It was not long before other countries followed their example, and today hardly a week goes by without some kind of dog show somewhere in the country.

Right: A day at a show can be very tiring. This Yorkshire Terrier is snoozing in the ring

Jack Russell Terrier

The importance of dog shows

Dog shows are the canine equivalent of beauty competitions. In a dog show, pedigree dogs are evaluated against the official breed standard by special judges. These standards are published by the breed society of the breed's country of origin or the relevant national kennel club.

The breed standard describes exactly what the finest possible example of the breed should look like. Some aspects of the breed are illustrated by line drawings.
Not only the height, the coat, and colour but also, for example, the shape of the head, the feet, and the ears are frequently described in great detail.

This show is being held in a beautiful location: Longchamps in Paris

In many cases, a particular breed's faults are also listed and the extent to which these should be penalised by the judges. Anyone who has read a breed standard will know that they are not always very clear. Frequently they are couched in specialist terms and there may inadvertently be room for different interpretations.

Were every breeder independently to breed dogs according to the breed standard, it would still be possible for the same breed to have many differences in appearance. That is why the judge's role is so important.

The judge is responsible for interpreting the breed standard. He or she frequently has had a lot of experience with the breed in question. The judge therefore ensures the breed's homogeneity and its general behavioural destabilisation.

This Dogue d' Argentine is very fond of his owner

Since all breeders are naturally proud when a dog of theirs wins a class, the judges' opinion will play an important part in their choice of stud dogs.

Judges necessarily have a great deal of responsibility. The dogs they declare the winners will put their stamp on the coming generations of the breed.

However, shows are not only important in ensuring a breed's uniformity. They are also necessary for the maintenance and preservation of lesser-known breeds.

If a breeder of a lesser-known dog cannot sell his or her puppies, the breed will eventually die out. Shows give these breeders the opportunity to show their dogs to the public, there-by making them better known. For that matter, shows are not just for breeders and their dogs but also for the public.

A large dog show is the only place where people can see all the different breeds of dog collected together and talk to the breeders and enthusiasts about their dogs.

Procedure

Taking part in a dog show is, for most people and for their dogs, a nerve-wracking experience. Although the actual judging usually takes only a few moments, both the dog and the owner are expected to attend the show for the whole day.

There is, by and large, little money to be won: shows generally confer club titles or, by winning a number of competitions, the dogs may qualify for the coveted title of National Champion.

To make sure that promising young dogs that generally have not developed such a good coat or build as their adult breed companions do not go unrecognised, there are special classes for young dogs.

The best bitch and the best dog in both the puppy and adult classes can be considered for the winning title, but only one can be the breed champion.

This Alaskan Malamute is an excellent example of his breed

The Lowchen owes his name to the way he is trimmed to look like a lion

This standard Poodle has just won an important title

Where a number of different breeds are judged, the best examples of each breed will be judged against the best dogs of other, similar breeds. The best examples of the different breed groups finally complete for the title 'Best in Show'.

Ring training

There are few dogs that can perform well in the ring without some form of training.

If the dog doesn't present itself well because, for example, it is somewhat in awe of all the attention, it cannot be easily judged, and this

will influence the result. Similarly, dogs that are disobedient and do not stand when the judge wishes will not do very well.

Experienced dog showers know this. Their dogs should be very obedient in the ring and they have often prepared for the show for months. To show dogs successfully, a good relationship between owner or handler and dog is essential.

In Europe, dogs are usually shown by their owners or by someone else who deals with the dog on a daily basis, but in the United States there are professional 'handlers' who are expert at showing dogs.

These 'handlers' usually started to show other people's dogs at a very young age and have thereby gained a great deal of experience. The

The coat of a Bearded Collie requires a lot of care

Here are the biggest and the smallest Poodle types:
the toy and the standard. Poodles can be white, black,
brown, apricot, or grey, and do not moult

Afghan Hounds are remarkably handsome aristocratic
dogs. Their coat requires a great deal of attention

best of them can earn a good living out of this.

Of course, not everyone who wants to show their dog knows what will be required. This is why it is a good idea to go to watch a dog show once or twice to see what the dogs, their owners, and the judges do. However, this may not be enough, and it is sensible to ask your dog's breeder whether your dog has the potential to do well in a show.

A breeder who has confidence in his dogs will be happy to assist you and may even be disappointed if you decide not to show your dog. Very promising dogs are sometimes sold on

condition that the dog will be shown at least once by its new owner. And the breeder will usually advise you to contact a good dog club. Other owners may insist that you never enter your dog in a show.

Almost all dog clubs regularly hold so-called 'ring training' sessions, where both the owner and the dog are trained in showing techniques.

This ring training is not only useful for the owner but the dog also learns to behave perfectly in the presence of other dogs.

Coton de Tuléar puppy

Welsh Springer spaniel

Irish Terriers can be quite
obstinate

Coat care

At shows dogs are judged on their appearance, so every dog, whatever his breed, should look its best.

A dog that is ill must not attend a show because it could infect the other dogs.
Bitches on heat are also not admitted because they could create havoc among the male dogs. All dogs are examined by a veterinary surgeon before they are permitted into the showground and, if there is any doubt, they are sent home.

At almost every show, there are a number of dogs worthy of the championship, so it is frequently very small details that make the difference. This is why it is important that the dogs are shown at their best.

Obviously the coat should be clean and have no trace of fleas or other pests. The dog's nails must be cut short or filed, his ears will need to be cleaned and his coat must be given

a last-minute polish. Short-haired breeds require little attention to their coats. It is usually enough just to give the dog a bath a few days before the show and to brush it well. Sometimes his coat may be given an extra shine with a little oil, which will be available from your breeder.

Long-haired or rough-coated breeds require more attention. With such breeds, the judge will look not only at the dog's build and way of moving, but also the quality and length of the coat. Most such breeds must be shown with their coats clipped in a particular way.

However beautiful a dog is, if it has not been clipped correctly or its coat does not have the required length or structure, it is unlikely to win. No dog is perfect, however, and by

Weimaraners were originally kept at the court of Weimar in Germany, which is how they got their name
For some time only aristocrats were permitted to own them

trimming its coat in a particular way it is possible to emphasise its strong points.

People who show their dogs often know this and take account of it when trimming their dogs. It is very difficult to win against dogs that have been professionally trimmed and cared for.

A dog that has been professionally presented and that has enjoyed the best coat care may win over a dog that is of a better quality but has been less expertly cared for and presented. Breeds where the coat is an important element of the standard are, among others, Poodles and the Lhasa Apso, but the quality of coat will also influence the judges' opinion with Terrier breeds and certain sheepdog breeds, such as the Old English Sheepdog.

Show temperament or not

Some people do not show their dogs because they think that dogs do not like shows. There are certainly dogs who do not enjoy it and who dislike all the fuss and attention. Their attitude and body language will make this quite clear. As the dog needs to show itself at its best in the ring, unwilling dogs will generally not do well and will have only a short show career. But there are also dogs who stand immobile in the ring, proud and self-assured, with pricked ears, clearly enjoying all the attention.

This kind of dog is said to have the ideal 'show temperament'. The owner or handler has little to do to bring out the best in him. The dog shows himself.
Not infrequently such dogs remain champions for years. You can therefore rest assured that good show dogs really enjoy the whole business.

Winners

The winners in a dog show are handsome examples of their breeds. However, working ability is not judged in a beauty competition. Dogs with conformation faults that would prevent them doing the work for which they were bred rarely win. Whether they are intel-

Chow-Chow

Short-haired Collie

The Keeshond is a watchful companion

Italian Greyhound

ligent and willing enough, however, to do this work cannot be judged in a show.

Winning many shows says little about a dog's character and working ability. If you are looking for a dog to work, you would do well to buy a puppy from a litter whose parents have won work prizes.

In some countries, working dogs, which include some gun dogs and hounds, can only win championships if they have not only done well in a dog show but have also proved themselves in the field.

Such a system is greatly to be welcomed, although it does make it more difficult for breeders to breed champions.

CHAPTER 11

Popular breeds

For various reasons, some breeds of dog are obviously much more popular than others. Take a look at a favourite dog-walking area. This will give you quite a good idea of the most popular breeds of the moment. Most breeds are only at the top of the popularity stakes for a few years. Thereafter they have to make way for others. Some breeds, on the other hand, retain their popularity regardless of fashion.

Influence of the media

You may ask how it is that some breeds suddenly become enormously popular while other breeds, which might be much better suited as family pets, are forgotten. The media appears to have an important influence on the popularity of pedigree dogs.

For example, the popularity of the Collie increased by leaps and bounds in the years during which the 'Lassie' TV series and films were shown around the world. Everyone wanted to own an intelligent and beautiful dog that seemed almost human. The charming Disney cartoon '101 Dalmatians' in turn cast the spotlight on the Dalmatian and ensured that this breed became very popular.

In a similar way, a number of TV series, such as 'Magnum PI' (Dobermanns) and 'Jake and the Fat Man' (Bulldogs), have played an important part in bringing these breeds to the public's notice. In recent years the makers of

Jack Russell Terriers

English Cocker Spaniels

advertisements have added their influence by showing beautiful films featuring various dogs. The brief, highly romanticised pictures of different breeds encourage people to become dog owners themselves. Breed societies are frequently asked whether they know someone who has a litter of puppies 'like the one in the advertisement'.

Disadvantages of popularity

The popularity that overtakes many breeds is not necessarily a good thing. Many people will buy a pedigree dog out of impulse without enquiring about its background, needs, or character. In this way, an active sporting dog can end up in a small apartment and become neurotic through lack of exercise. Dogs whose coats need a great deal of care end up with people who have not given this any thought. The results of such thoughtless behaviour can be seen regularly in the newspapers.

There are far too many advertisements which include the words: 'due to unforeseen circumstances, a good home is sought for ... '
Dogs homes also contain many pedigree dogs that have suffered inappropriate treatment. Unscrupulous breeders seek to satisfy the demand by breeding large numbers of puppies. They do not care whether the parent dogs are really healthy, of a good pedigree, or

have a nice character, build or appearance. Puppies always look charming and will be sold to people who know no better. Without a hint of remorse, such breeders transfer their activities to another breed when the first begins to become less popular. At a time of huge popularity, many good and serious breeders may stop breeding precisely because they cannot bear to see the decline in quality of their beloved breed.

The standard of the foundation stock for breeding future generations then becomes unpredictable. More than once a breed that is hugely popular with children suddenly proves to have a number of dogs that are aggressive or that suffer from some hereditary disease or weakness which may cost a great deal to put right. Alternatively, however, popularity managed properly gives breeder the chance to work with a bigger gene pool and selectively breed out undesirable inheritable physical or behaviour problems.

Too much popularity may be bad for any breed, and a prospective dog owner would do well to talk to the breed society before buying a popular breed. Breed societies do their best to give the public sound information and to warn them against dangers.

Breed societies are there to help – ask the Kennel Club for details of the appropriate

Bulldog

societies. Many societies now advertise in dog magazines and newspapers, and are easily accessible to the general public.

Popular dogs

The dogs discussed below have all been popular for some time, so you are likely to know most of them.

St Bernard

The St Bernard is a well-known breed. Its origins are in Switzerland where it was bred by monks to rescue travellers who had become lost or perhaps injured.

St Bernards are considered to be quiet dogs, but there are many enthusiastic and highly active specimens as well. They can be short or long coated.
St Bernards need a lot of space and, like all dogs, must have a very well-balanced diet in order to become strong and healthy.

English Cocker Spaniel

The English Cocker Spaniel is an old sporting breed, principally used to hunt birds. Cocker Spaniels are very gentle and friendly dogs, and most can be trained to get on well with children. They are intelligent and quickly learn

Long-haired Dachshund

new commands, but some evidence shows that the self-coloured dogs can be difficult when young.

Cocker Spaniels love water and will not pass a ditch or pond without wanting to jump in.

Bulldog

Since the TV series 'Jake and the Fat Man', interest in Bulldogs has increased considerably.

Bulldogs are sensitive, agreeable companions, with almost human expressions. They are very affectionate and feel happiest when they can be part of a family. Although it is fierce in appearance, the Bulldog is warm and affectionate.

The breed is friendly, sociable, easy to deal with, and rarely barks. Their characteristic physique, however, means that they cannot manage long walks and they are also not very happy in high temperatures, when they will find it difficult to breathe.

Keeshond

Keeshonds are familiar pets whose popularity has waned somewhat. They come in three sizes: toy, medium, and large.
The best-known is undoubtedly the toy Keeshond, while the medium-sized animal is seen least often.

Berner Sennert

Keeshonds are pleasant and obedient companions, with a watchful character. They are generally very territorial, so they rarely roam.

Bernese Mountain Dog

Bernese Mountain Dogs are very popular family dogs. In their country of origin, Switzerland, they were used for all sorts of tasks, including hauling and guarding.

They are handsome dogs, with a quiet and reliable character. Generally they are sociable and friendly, but they are also very good guard dogs. If necessary they will defend their family against attack.

Bernese Mountain Dogs are large dogs and grow quickly.
They need good care while they are growing and there should be no economising on the quality of their food. As with all dogs, Bernese Mountain Dogs do well with kindly, consistent training.

Dachshunds

There will be few people who do not know the Dachshund by name. Their very affectionate though independent and brave nature and unusual appearance have led to these dogs long-term popularity.

Dobermann

There are three sizes of Dachshund: standard, miniature, and Kaninchen.

The standard Dachshund is, as the name suggests, the largest and original size; the miniature is somewhat smaller; and the Kaninchen (which means 'rabbit') Dachshund is the smallest of the three. Dachshunds come not only in three sizes but also in three varieties of coat: short-haired, long-haired, and wire-haired.

The short-haired is the original Dachshund and some twenty years ago was the most popular variety.

The wire-haired Dachshund, which has been very popular in recent years, was developed by crossing with the less well-known Dandie Dinmont Terrier.

The short- and wire-haired Dachshunds are the keenest hunters, and their independent nature means that their training requires greater insight and expertise. The long-haired Dachshund is generally considered to be the most friendly and obliging of the Dachshunds. This is probably because of his Spaniel and Setter ancestry. Dachshunds are generally healthy, robust dogs. They are not always very obedient but with loving and consistent training you can teach them the basics. Dachshunds have weak spines and it is therefore

Rottweilers have been in the top ten most popular breeds for years

Boxer

not advisable to ask a Dachshund to walk up and down stairs, or to ask him to jump.

Dachshunds need regular exercise and a good diet. Be careful not to offer too many snacks which may cause it to put on weight. Being overweight is bad for any dog, but for the Dachshund – with its long back – it is particularly dangerous.

Rottweiler

Rottweilers have been in the top ten of popular breeds for years. Nevertheless they are far from ideal for everybody. These dogs can be dominant and aggressive, and need a firm and affectionate environment. Rottweilers are very fond of their own family and can be great playmates for the children.

All Rottweilers have a strong instinct to protect their people as well as the house and grounds. They are unshakeably loyal.

Rottweilers are best in a harmonious family where they are given clear leadership. The breed generally does very well in training competitions. They are reliable and enthusiastic workers, although occasionally somewhat slower in the uptake than, for example, sheepdogs.

A big advantage, however, is their tremendous memory; what they have once learned they will never forget.

Irish Setter

In recent years, the popularity of the Irish Setter has dwindled. For many years this beautiful breed with its deep-red coat was incredibly popular. Irish Setters were originally bred to hunt birds, but recently they have not been used much for hunting. The Irish Setter is a very gentle, friendly and sociable dog but can also be incredibly obstinate.

Maltese Terrier

The Maltese Terrier, sometimes erroneously called the Maltese Lion, is a very popular breed. It is certainly the most well known of the Bichon group to which he belongs. Maltese Terriers are playful and very obedient dogs.

They are always cheerful and like people. Their gentle and uncomplicated character makes them suitable for people with less experience of dog training, and they will rarely take offence. The shining silky-white coat of the Maltese requires a great deal of care. It is very difficult to keep it in perfect condition. Many people, therefore, choose to have it cut short several times a year in a dog parlour.

Rough Collie. The dog is sable and white: the most frequent colour combination

These three beauties are American Cocker Spaniels

At dog shows, however, much value is placed on the quality and length of the coat and show dogs will likely need to be professionally groomed.

American Cocker Spaniel

The American Cocker Spaniel comes in many different self-coloured and broken-coated varieties. The coat of this breed needs a great deal of care, as do their ears which should be checked regularly.

American Cocker Spaniels are unusually co-operative, sensitive, and playful animals that need gentle training. They are very adaptable and, as long as they have regular exercise, can be completely happy in a flat. The American Cocker Spaniels were developed from the English Cocker Spaniel.

'Lady', from the Disney classic 'The Lady and the Tramp', was an American Cocker Spaniel.

Jack Russell Terrier

The Jack Russell Terrier has recently been recognised as a separate breed. Now that the dogs are being registered, it appears that in many countries these courageous Terriers have already become one of the top twenty most popular breeds.

The Jack Russell was bred by Parson Russell,

Keeshound

who lived and worked in Devon in the early nineteenth century. Because he was less interested in the appearance of the dogs than in their ability to work, there are even now many different kinds of Jack Russell Terrier.

The Jack Russell was, and is, much in vogue with the horsey set since he will enthusiastically and quickly rid stables of mice and other vermin. Jack Russells require a great deal of exercise and activity.

Their temperament is far too lively to be happy with just a warm place by the fire.
The Jack Russell is an independent and very courageous dog that has a great deal of initiative.

Nevertheless, it is an excellent playmate for children.

Long-haired Dachshund

Bernese Mountain Dog

doors and garden gates by watching people do it. Dobermanns can be very determined and are excellent guard dogs.

The Dobermann is a courageous, strong, and very affectionate animal that likes to be in the vicinity of its owner. Nevertheless, a Dobermann is not the right dog for every family. It needs a peaceful environment and it is important that its owner and the other members of the family are extremely consistent. The Dobermann needs to be carefully trained when young.

Dobermann

The Dobermann, also known as the Dobermann Pinscher, is a sharp dog with a great deal of character and many uses. The Dobermann is the creation of Louis Dobermann, a tax-collector in the mid-nineteenth century who sought a dog who could accompany him on his daily round.

He wanted a dog that would be not only agile, obedient, clever and courageous, but also beautiful. The breeds he used to create the Dobermann is a secret he took to his grave, but it is assumed that the Manchester Terrier, the German Pinscher, and possibly a mastiff or greyhound-like dog will have formed part of the chosen mix. The Dobermann excels in a number of canine sports, and as a breed is intelligent, eager to learn and also very crafty: it is the kind of dog that learns how to open

In some European countries it is no longer permitted to crop this dog's ears, but with or without ears, it remains the same pleasant companion with a pronounced character.

Belgian Shepherd Dogs

Belgian Shepherd Dogs have been firm favourites as family and sporting dogs for many years. The short-haired Malinois type in particular is used a great deal in competitive training. Malinois are courageous and very fast. The Tervueren Shepherd Dog and the Groenendael Shepherd Dog are the long-haired varieties of these sheepdogs. These two breeds may be more gentle, but they are certainly not timid.

They are very active dogs, with considerable endurance, and enjoy long walks and all sorts of other activities. Most of them are good retrievers and love swimming.

West Highland White Terriers

The Laeken Shepherd Dog is the rough-coated variety. Although this breed is less known, it has a firm core of enthusiastic fans in Europe.

All Belgian Shepherd Dogs need a lot of exercise and are at their best in an active family.

Boxer

The Boxer is a German breed, descended from the Brabant Bullbiter that used to be very popular as a bull-fighting dog. The Boxer is far more friendly than his fierce ancestor. They are very lively, enthusiastic family dogs, that are happy to come out of their basket to play or to run about.

In light of their athletic build, this is hardly surprising. They are well known for being good with children. However, they are also good guard dogs; a Boxer will always protect its territory and people against marauders and will not give in easily. They are also very intelligent and learn relatively quickly.
Despite the fact that they can be very playful and too easily distracted, Boxers are used both as guide dogs and police dogs in many countries.

Labrador Retriever

The Labrador Retriever has been a very well-known and popular dog for many years. It was originally a gun dog and continues to have a large following among hunters.

Labrador Retrievers are intelligent, obedient, and eager to learn, and are, in general, quite calm.
Worldwide they are used for all sorts of jobs, from assisting the blind to locating drugs. They also do very well in obedience tests and in other forms of dog sport.

Labrador Retrievers are friendly family dogs that get along well with everybody and usually love children and other pets. They love swimming and need lots of exercise.

Rough or Smooth Collie

The Rough or Smooth Collie is a Scottish sheepdog breed that is better known as the 'Lassie' dog. Lassie was the name of the world-

Belgian Shepherds

famous Rough Collie that kept people glued to the TV watching his heroic deeds.

Everyone wanted such an intelligent heroic dog, and for a time, the Rough Collie was extremely popular. Excessive popularity was not good for the Rough Collie, and many ended up in dogs homes because they did not fulfil the romantic image people had of the breed.

It is amusing to note that, although 'Lassie' means 'girl', all of the dogs that played Lassie over the years were male dogs and should therefore have been 'Laddies' rather than 'Lassies'.

Fortunately for the Rough Collie, its popularity has waned somewhat and it now enjoys only a healthy amount of interest.

This Belgian Shepherd Dog (Groenendael) is shaking himself after swimming

These Bouvier puppies will become imposing guard dogs

This intelligent and sensitive dog is an excellent family dog. It is very loyal and very attentive to his owner. The Rough Collies is particularly gentle and protective of children, but will require a certain amount of grooming. Collies are good watchdogs, usually easy to train and very clean.

Collies can be Rough- or Smooth-coated and come in three colours. Sable and white is the most frequently seen; another colour is tricolour, which is principally black, with white and tan markings. Collies can also be blue merle: a light, silver blue with black markings.

Golden Retriever

In many countries, the Golden Retriever has become one of the most popular breeds. Originally a gun dog, there are many hunters who have remained loyal to the breed despite its popularity.

Golden Retrievers are intelligent and quick learners. Friendly and out-going, they get on with all members of the family, including the children.

They love swimming and long walks. Although a Golden Retriever's coat requires little care, it may need to visit a dog parlour once or twice a year to have its coat trimmed.

This Yorkshire Terrier shows what the coat of a good show dog should be like

The German Shepherd Dogs have a large number of uses. They are used not only to track escaped prisoners but also to sniff out marijuana and heroin. They serve as rescue dogs, guide dogs and police dogs. The German Shepherd Dog loves his family, is watchful, makes a good guard dog, and is not inclined to roam. It makes no sense to keep this dog in a kennel; it lives for the attention and approval of its owner.

The prospective owner of a German Shepherd Dog will have to consider the fact that as a breed they require a great deal of attention and exercise.

West Highland White Terrier

The West Highland White Terrier, 'Westie' for short, has grown in popularity over recent years. These charming, courageous, and sharp little dogs are closely related to the Cairn Terrier, which is also becoming more popular.

Westies need firm and consistent handling when young as they can be obstinate and very naughty. Most people have difficulty being strict with these dogs, because of their appearance. Westies like being busy; they enjoy digging, and will retrieve balls and toys with great enthusiasm.

They are generally good with children – although because they are self-reliant and wilful, they may not be an easy first dog. They are not prepared to put up with a lazy life and are therefore best suited to an active family.
Their coat needs careful attention and it is a good idea to take the dog to the dog parlour regularly.
West Highland White Terriers should be washed as little as possible because washing tends to make the coat too soft.

German Shepherd Dog

German Shepherd Dogs are among the best-known and loved dogs in the world. There was a time when they were almost too popular.

Cavalier King Charles Spaniel

The Cavalier King Charles Spaniel is an old sporting breed. Its friendly, exuberant, and obliging nature has stolen the heart of many enthusiasts.

The dog takes its name from Charles II, who made no secret of his love for the breed. The type we now know was almost extinct at the beginning of this century. Breeders preferred

Maltese Terriers

Golden Retrievers

to keep the long coat in good condition. Not surprisingly, therefore, this very popular little dog is usually seen with a short coat. Not all Yorkshire Terriers are able to develop such a long coat, however much care the owner takes of it.

The puppies are always born with smooth black coats which become lighter with time. For this reason, it is difficult to predict a puppy's eventual coat colour. Yorkshire Terriers are full of character, sporty, and cheerful dogs that are also very observant and make good guards. They are intelligent and lively and very affectionate.

the flat faces of the Pekinese and the Japanese Spaniel and crossed these dogs with the Cavalier King Charles in the hope that this breed would also get a flat face.

The descendants of these crosses are now a distinct breed, the King Charles Spaniel. The short-nosed Spaniels became so popular that the original type almost became extinct. However, a number of enthusiasts managed to save the breed.

The Cavalier is cheerful and pleasant family dog.

Bouvier des Flandres
Bouviers are imposing guard dogs. This Belgian breed was used for years as a cattle herder, but is now better known as a guard dog.
Nevertheless Bouviers are pleasant and loyal family dogs that are generally good with children.

Yorkshire Terrier
The coat of a Yorkshire Terrier must be long and shiny if you wish it to take part in a dog show. It is almost impossible for most people

German Shepherd

Lesser-known breeds

Many breeds of dog deserve a little more of the spotlight. It is to everyone's advantage if the demand for puppies is spread equally across all breeds. In this chapter, some less popular breeds will receive some well-earned attention.

Most people know only a relatively small number of breeds of dog. People who do not own a dog and may even have no interest in dogs will probably be able to name a German Shepherd Dog or a Golden Retriever. These breeds occur so frequently that there will almost certainly be someone among their family and friends who has such a dog.

Most prospective dog owners who are facing the difficult task of choosing among the large number of breeds available still tend to choose one of the better-known breeds. This is, of course, a pity.

There are so many other breeds that are more suitable as family dogs. Some breeds are now so rare that they are threatened with extinction. The breeders of these dogs do what they can to keep the breed going, but it is not easy with so little encouragement. Other breeds are well known among people who show their dogs and who have a specialised interest but they are unknown among the general public.

North American White Shepherds

Breeders of these dogs will only breed a litter if there is enough interest to guarantee that they can sell the puppies. You will rarely see puppies advertised in your local paper; the puppies are usually already spoken for before the litter is born.

You may ask why these breeds are so little known. Are they ugly? Or do they have certain weaknesses or character faults which make them less suitable as household pets? Are they unhealthy, or so expensive that they are not affordable for the average household? In most cases, the opposite is true. Many lesser-known breeds are excellent pets with charming characters and most attractive appearances.

Lesser-known breeds

If the demand for puppies was spread more among the breeds, the somewhat dubious trade in popular breeds would diminish and interesting and unusual breeds would be saved for future generations.

Serious breeders, pedigree dogs and future dog owners would all come out as winners. The following are some of the breeds that ought to be better known.

Austrian Pinscher
Few people will know the Austrian Pinscher. These dogs were originally kept as farmyard dogs in Austria and they took on not only the task of guarding the farm, but also acting as talented vermin exterminators.

They are watchful dogs that are extremely fond of their family, so they have difficulty getting used to a new owner.

Shiba Inu
The Shiba Inu is an extremely old Japanese breed. It appears that dogs of this breed have assisted the Japanese in the hunt for over 2000

Austrian Pinscher. This is a good example of the breed

years. They were praised not only as hunting dogs but also as guard dogs and companions. As Shiba Inus greatly resemble the Chinese Wolf and Asian Pariah Dogs, it is probable that their origins must lie in China. At some point they must have reached Japan in the company of travellers and nomads, where they are now greatly prized.

The Japanese government is very strict about its national breeds of dog, which include not only the Shiba Inu but also the Japanese Akita and the Tosa Inu. These breeds are protected in Japan and their purity is jealously guarded. Shiba Inus are intelligent, cheerful, and energetic little dogs.

They bark little and are most adaptable.

Although they are very fond of their owner and family, they do not follow their owner around all day. Their characters are much too independent.

Chihuahua

The Chihuahua is the world's smallest breed. It comes from Mexico, where it was bred and kept by the Tolteks, and later by the Aztecs, for various purposes. The main reason in keeping these small, brave dogs was religious.

Today the Chihuahua is an affectionate, companionable little guard dog with a healthy public following.
Chihuahuas are either smooth- or long-coated and come in all sorts of colours.

Nova Scotia Duck Tolling Retriever

The Nova Scotia Duck Tolling Retriever is a middle-sized American breed, principally used to hunt ducks. In addition, it is a delightful family dog.

The breed is notable for its red colour and intelligent obliging character. They are good with other dogs and pets, and are a real companion for the whole family. Tollers like working for their owners and enjoy taking part in various forms of canine sport, such as agility and flyball.

Eurasier

The Eurasier is a recent German breed. The aim was to create the ideal house dog with the appearance and watchfulness of the Keeshond and that would only raise the alarm if really necessary.

The Chihuahua is the smallest breed in the world

Nova Scotia Duck Tolling Retriever

Dandie Dinmont Terriers

The breed was developed from Keeshonds, Chow Chows, and Samoyeds. Eurasiers are very loyal household pets with a calm and uncomplicated character.

They are also very adaptable which makes them suitable for families in small houses. The Eurasier comes in many different colours.

Dandie Dinmont Terrier

The Dandie Dinmont Terrier was one of the breeds used to develop the rough-coated Dachshund. Dandie Dinmonts are a very old hunting dog. In England, their country of origin, they were used to hunt small game such as rabbits.

Sir Walter Scott, the famous novelist, wrote a novel in which a farmer, Dandie Dinmont, played a prominent part. This farmer frequently hunted with his long-legged, rough-coated dogs called Pepper and Mustard. The novel was widely read and caused tremendous popularity for the 'Dandie Dinmont Terrier'.

Today this unusual-looking Terrier is rarely seen outside England. Dandie Dinmont Terriers are particularly courageous hunters.

They are also good pets. They are very loyal dogs with a somewhat independent, though charming, character.

Bedlington Terrier

The Bedlington Terrier is also known as the 'wolf in sheep's clothing'. Although with his curly coat the Bedlington Terrier may look like a sheep, it is anything but: these dogs have very strong characters. These middle-sized,

Eurasier

This striking dog is an example of an old Irish gun dog, the Irish Water Spaniel

active, unusual-looking dogs have a small but loyal following. The Bedlington Terrier was not only used for hunting but was also used as a guard dog.

In addition, it was used for racing. The Bedlington has the same ancestor as the Dandie Dinmont Terrier, the now extinct Rothbury Terrier, but it also has a lot of Whippet blood.

It is a courageous and companionable guard that is very attached to his own people and rather reserved with strangers.

Shar Pei

The Shar Pei is a Chinese breed that has, over time, performed a number of different tasks. In some respects, its similarity to the Chow Chow is unmistakable.

Young Shar Peis have a great many wrinkles in their skin, but adult dogs may only be moderately wrinkled. Once this breed was extremely rare almost to the point of being

Left: Cesky Terrier

Below left: The Bedlington Terrier is also known as a "wolf in sheep's clothing"

Below: Anybody coming across a Mexican Hairless Dog or Xoloitzcuintli, Xolo for short, will stop and stare at his extraordinary appearance

Sussex Spaniel

extinct, but nowadays examples are seen more frequently. Shar Peis are unusual and delightful family dogs, but because of their rather dominant character they do require a firm owner and great consistency in their training.

Cesky Terrier
In 1950 in Czechoslovakia, a man by the name of Horak wanted to develop a vermin-hunting dog by crossing Scottish Terriers and Sealyham Terriers.

These two breeds were a little too heavily built for his taste, and he therefore selected the most lightly built examples for his breeding programme. Nowadays the Cesky Terrier weighs between 6 and 9kg (13 and 20lb). Cesky Terriers, also known as Bohemian Terriers, are very playful and intelligent dogs with a friendly character.

The Cesky Terrier does not moult but does need to be brushed regularly. The breed is shown at dog shows with a special trim: the back, the neck, and the side of the head are cut short, while the coat underneath the stomach, on the chest, and on the head remains long.

These dogs are striking, not least on account of their unusual colours and the silky shine on their coats.

North American White Shepherd Dog
The North American White Shepherd is in fact no more than a white German Shepherd Dog. In the past, a white German Shepherd Dog was not unique: there were frequently white puppies in many litters.

Nevertheless, over time, the white dogs were considered less desirable and were no longer taken to shows or used for breeding. Although a number of enthusiasts remained faithful to this colour, those against it won the day. The result is that the White Shepherd Dog is still not recognised as a breed, although it does now enjoy a growing number of enthusiasts and breeders.

The North American White Shepherd Dog is an intelligent dog with a great ability to learn. It does very well in various forms of canine sport, is sociable and is an ideal com-panion for the whole family. In addition, it is good with other dogs and pets.

Irish Water Spaniel
The Irish Water Spaniel is an old Irish hunting breed. Irish Water Spaniels were used to retrieve ducks and other water game. His coat is somewhat oily, which protects the dog against the cold when swimming, but which gives them a characteristic and quite strong odour.

Irish Water Spaniels are always liver-coloured. Also typical of the breed is the short coat on the head and the tail.
Irish Water Spaniels are very intelligent dogs that are quick to learn new commands if they are trained properly.

Just like all Irish dogs, the Irish Water Spaniel can also be obstinate and independent. So they need careful handling when young.

This young bitch is an example of a Venezuelan breed, the Mucuchies

Bergamasco

The Bergamasco is a very striking and rare dog. It is an Italian breed that is much prized in Italy.

They are independent guard dogs that are still used to guard and herd cattle and to protect the herds against marauders. The body of an adult Bergamasco is covered by a thick blanket of matted strands of hair. Only the hair on the head and the shoulders does not have this tendency to mat.

The Bergamasco is happiest in surroundings that enable it to take its own initiative. It takes its job as guard dog very seriously.
Bergamascos are intelligent and fairly large dogs, the average height at the shoulder being 58cm (23in).

Glen of Imaal Terrier

The Glen of Imaal Terrier always looks smaller in a photograph than in reality. Anyone seeing this dog for the first time may be surprised by the dog's proportions, power and sheer mass.

Nevertheless the average shoulder height is no more than 35cm (14in). Sadly, few people have the opportunity to see this dog in real life as it has become very rare.

The Glen of Imaal Terrier originally comes from Ireland where it was used on farms to catch vermin, and as a reliable guard dog. In addition, this breed was used for hunting. Now the Glen of Imaal Terrier is better known as a characterful companion that is at its best in a fairly active family.

At any suggestion of a threat, the dog will let out its very deep bark. Despite its many positive qualities, this dog is not for everyone. It needs very firm, though affectionate, training. In his youth it will also need to be very carefully socialised in order to develop into a friendly and sociable dog.
They are very reserved with people whom they do not know.

Sussex Spaniel

The Sussex Spaniel is a fairly heavily built dog with a striking colour. Its coat is liver-coloured with a golden shine. In the past the Sussex was used for hunting.
They were slow but reliable workers who flushed out the birds so that hunters could shoot them. Once the bird had been killed, they retrieved it and brought it back to the hunter.

The Sussex was very popular before the turn of the century, but unfortunately other Spaniel breeds have overtaken it and as a result the breed has almost disappeared. The few remaining breeders face difficulties because the Sussex occurs so rarely it is not easy to find good breeding dogs.

The Sussex Spaniel is a friendly, charming dog that sometimes can be very independent and disobedient. It does, however, make a very good household pet that gets along well with everybody.

Japanese Chin

The Japanese Chin or Japanese Spaniel is a little-known breed. Originally Chinese, this dog gained popularity in Japan when it was introduced to court.

This dog was briefly very fashionable in England and today is firmly established here. The Japanese Chin is a small companion dog with a silky coat that needs little attention. They are gentle, cheerful dogs that like company. Not more than 25cm (10in) at the shoulder, most of the breed is black and white, but red and white is also acceptable.

Mexican Hairless Dog

Anyone encountering a Mexican Hairless Dog will stop and stare at its strange appearance. This breed originated in Mexico where archaeological digs have shown that hairless dogs have been known for over 2000 years.

These remarkable-looking dogs get their name from the Aztec god Xoloth. They have been nicknamed 'Xolos', and they come in two sizes: up to 59cm (23in) at the shoulder and not more than 33cm (13in) at the shoulder. The big advantage of these dogs is that their skin does not attract fleas, they do not smell, and their skin requires little attention. However, unless it is regularly scrubbed and oiled the skin will quickly age and harden.

Xolos are quiet dogs that bark only when there is something seriously wrong. Although they love attention, they are wary of strangers and tend to be one-person dogs. Litters of these dogs will occasionally produce hairy puppies, but they are not recognised by kennel clubs in all countries.

Chinese Crested Dog

It has been suggested that the history of the Chinese Crested Dog is similar to that of the Mexican Hairless Dog, and that it originated in Mexico, although it was finally discovered in China.

Others argue that both dogs were developed from the hairless dogs of Africa. The Chinese Crested Dog is better known than the Mexican Hairless. The hairy variety of the Chinese Crested, known as the 'Powder Puff', is recognised in dog shows around the world and is also used for breeding. The Chinese Crested has less pigmentation than the Mexican Hairless and therefore burns more easily in the sun. Sun-protection cream is no luxury on a sunny day.

Their soft, supple skin is much prized in show dogs. Chinese Crested Dogs are lively, intelligent, and good watch dogs.

Mucuchies

The Mucuchies is a Venezuelan breed that is principally found in the Andes, where farmers use them not only to herd flocks but also as guard dogs.

The breed is virtually unknown elsewhere in the world and consequently not recognised by any kennel clubs. There are many other breeds that are well known locally where they perform particular functions, but have not been discovered by dog lovers.

Chinese Hound

This breed, also known as the Thai Ridgeback, originated in an area stretching from Kashmir, through Thailand, to China, where they have been used as hunting and guard dogs. They are rarely seen elsewhere.

A characteristic of the breed is the ridge of hair along the back which grows in the opposite direction to the rest of the coat. The colours are black, blue, silver, and tan, with a short and velvety coat. They make good household pets, becoming very attached to their own people and generally behaving well with other dogs.

Index

Photo Credits

Sandra Arts   p. 84 below left

C.C. Asselbergs   p. 91 below right

Chris Eisenga   p. 8 above,
p. 54 above right

Kiddo bv   p. 111

R. van Riet en
H. Vrieze   p. 76 below left

Royal Canin bv   p. 110 above right,
p. 106 above

**Esther J.J. Verhoef-
Verhallen**   all other photos